THE LADY OF BELMONT

THE
LADY OF BELMONT

A PLAY IN FIVE ACTS

BY
ST. JOHN G. ERVINE

New York
THE MACMILLAN COMPANY
1924

Printed in Great Britain

TO

LAWRENCE LANGNER

THE FIRST ACT

A room, opening off a courtyard, in PORTIA's house in Belmont.
Early evening.

THE SECOND ACT

Same as Act I.   Two hours later.

THE THIRD ACT

A hall in PORTIA's house.   Three hours later.

THE FOURTH ACT

A bedroom in the house of LORENZO and JESSICA in Belmont.
Two hours later.

THE FIFTH ACT

The garden of PORTIA's house in Belmont.
The next morning.

The time is exactly ten years after the date of ANTONIO'S
Trial in " The Merchant of Venice."

The entire action of the play takes place in less than twenty-
four hours.

CHARACTERS

PORTIA, a rich lady of Belmont, wife to BASSANIO.

NERISSA, formerly her maid, wife to GRATIANO.

JESSICA, SHYLOCK'S daughter and wife to LORENZO.

BASSANIO, a Venetian, living in Belmont.

ANTONIO, a retired merchant of Venice, living near BASSANIO.

DOCTOR BELLARIO, a lawyer of Padua and cousin to PORTIA.

GRATIANO
LORENZO } Venetian friends of BASSANIO, living in Belmont.

YOUNG LORENZO, son to JESSICA and LORENZO.

LAUNCELOT GOBBO, LORENZO'S servant.

BALTHASAR, PORTIA'S steward.

STEPHANO, a young servant in PORTIA'S house.

SHYLOCK, a Jew of Venice.

A MESSENGER.

      Servants, retainers, guests, etc.

THE FIRST ACT

The scene is laid in a room opening off a courtyard in PORTIA'S *house in Belmont. A short flight of steps lead from it to the rest of the house. People entering from the courtyard descend a flight of broad steps. A heavy gate, giving access to the courtyard from the public road, is visible.*

The time is the early evening. The scene steadily darkens during the action so that at the end of the first act the courtyard is dark, except for the illuminations.

[*Enter* BALTHASAR, PORTIA'S *Steward, a man of pompous manner, conceited and humourless. He is followed by* NERISSA, *now a matronly figure, but hardly so genial as she was in " The Merchant of Venice." Her face bears the signs of continual anxiety. Life with* GRATIANO *has not been so full of entertainment as she had hoped it would be. She is now in a state of anger, which is not made any less by the manner of* BALTHASAR.]

BALTHASAR.   I will tell my mistress you are here, but I doubt if she will see you.   She is busy, and has much to do.

NERISSA.   Nevertheless, I wish to speak to her.

BALTHASAR.   You know her cousin comes to-day ?

NERISSA.   Cousin ! What cousin ?

BALTHASAR.   Doctor Bellario.

NERISSA.   The lawyer ?

BALTHASAR.   From Padua.   He has not been in this house for more than ten years.

NERISSA.   Doctor Bellario !   And is he friendly now to my lady ?

BALTHASAR.   I do not know whether he is friendly or not, but he is coming.

NERISSA (*cogitating*).   H'm ! I wonder what this means. Is it Bassanio who brings him here ?

BALTHASAR. I am a discreet man, madam.

NERISSA. Come, come, Balthasar, your discretion is well enough for those who are strange to you, but I know you are as fond of gossip as any man on earth, especially if it be spiteful.

BALTHASAR. I have some of the failings of humanity, madam! . . .

NERISSA. Well, then, tell me all. It *is* Bassanio that brings his lady's cousin here? Eh? Come, what's the trouble now?

BALTHASAR. I will tell my lady you are here.

NERISSA. You were in no hurry to tell her when I first came, and my message can wait a little longer. Oh, Balthasar, I am hungry for a scandalous conversation. Gratify me. It *is* Bassanio, is it not?

BALTHASAR. I fear my lady finds my lord importunate.

NERISSA. Importunate! In love?

BALTHASAR. Other ladies find him so, but his importunities to my mistress are not to her heart, but to her purse.

NERISSA. Indeed, I know. My husband! . . .

BALTHASAR. Have you come here to complain of Gratiano?

NERISSA. I have, God help me!

BALTHASAR. Then you may save your breath. My mistress is acquainted with your husband's habits, and does not like them. There is no spendthrift folly in which he and my lord Bassanio do not make a pair.

NERISSA. I'll thank you to leave my husband's habits to me, Balthasar. With all his faults, he is twice the man that you will ever be.

BALTHASAR. Perhaps, madam, the world does not share your opinion.

NERISSA. Your satisfaction with yourself, Balthasar, makes me feel exceedingly sick.

BALTHASAR. Better be sick, madam, with self-satisfaction than be sick, as you are, with disappointment. Here comes Antonio.

NERISSA. Don't leave me with him! He'll tell me again how near he was to losing his pound of flesh!

[*She turns to fly from the room, but* ANTONIO *enters from the courtyard before she has time to do so.*]

ANTONIO. Ah, my gentle Nerissa!

[ANTONIO *has aged considerably in the last ten years. He has a fretful, misunderstood manner, and his priggishness and pomposity are now lacking in the dignity which enabled him to carry off his grand signior ways in Venice.*]

NERISSA. Good-day to you, Antonio, sir.

ANTONIO. I have not seen you—how long?

NERISSA. A week. That's all. A short week.

ANTONIO. I am sure it is longer ago than that . . .

NERISSA. Only a week, Antonio. (*To* BALTHASAR.) I pray you, tell my lady I am here.

[BALTHASAR *goes into the house.*

ANTONIO. We are getting old, Nerissa, very old.

NERISSA. I do not feel myself so old.

ANTONIO. Oh, but you are, and getting older. One of these mornings, Nerissa, you will see your face in the glass, and you will know that you are old, very old. And some of your friends will say you should have discovered it long ago.

NERISSA. You are a comfortable companion, Antonio!

ANTONIO. I do not flatter. Why should I? No one flatters me. Do you know what day this is, Nerissa?

NERISSA. Yes! Wednesday!

ANTONIO. I do not mean a common, ordinary sort of a Wednesday. Think, Nerissa!

NERISSA. Why should one Wednesday be more than any other Wednesday? They are all Wednesdays to me.

ANTONIO. What a fickle thing is the memory of man! Why, Nerissa, on this day, ten years ago, my life was sought! . . .

NERISSA. I know the story well. I have heard it before.

ANTONIO. By Shylock, there in Venice. A Jew! God save us all, a Jew!

NERISSA. I wonder if it will rain to-night.

ANTONIO. Rain! Why should it rain?

NERISSA. I do not know. I wondered.

ANTONIO. You put me off my argument with your irrelevant speculations on weather. This Jew, Shylock, had a bond of me that I should lose a pound of flesh—flesh, mark you!—to be cut off by him nearest my heart if I should fail to pay him some three thousand ducats that he had lent Bassanio on my security.

NERISSA.   Indeed, Antonio, I know the story only too well.

ANTONIO.   A pound of flesh! Nearest my heart! Here! This very spot! I'll show it to you!

[*He begins to unfasten his doublet.*

NERISSA.   I beg you, no! I have seen it many times before, and I have a nervous heart.

ANTONIO (*doing his doublet up again*).   Well, then, you shall not see it. Do you think, Nerissa, I should have died if Shylock had had his bond?

NERISSA.   Perhaps! One never knows!

ANTONIO.   They tell me surgeons have great skill with flesh, and can undo a man and tie him up again and leave him better than he was. Some say we have too many organs inside us.

NERISSA.   I can well believe it!

ANTONIO.   I might have lived.

NERISSA.   Oh, no doubt of that!

ANTONIO.   I fear sometimes Bassanio does not remember how much he owes me. He is very careless with his friends.

NERISSA.   Aye, and with his wife and her fortune.

ANTONIO.   But not to remember his debt to me; that's ingratitude, Nerissa, gross ingratitude. A man may fail in circumspection to his wife and not be chid for it, but to fail his friend—and such a friend!—no, no, that's ingratitude! I nearly lost my life for him.

NERISSA.   And it was saved by Portia.

ANTONIO.   Yes, yes, of course, and I am grateful to her.

[*Re-enter* BALTHASAR. *As he does so,* LORENZO *comes into the courtyard.*]

BALTHASAR.   My lady bids me bring you to her chamber.

NERISSA.   I'll go at once. (*Enter* LORENZO.) Why Lorenzo, I thought you were gone to France.

LORENZO.   I am on my way, but have stopped to take leave of Portia. Good evening, Antonio!

ANTONIO. Good evening, good evening!

LORENZO (*to* BALTHASAR). Is she within?

BALTHASAR. She is, my lord. I'll tell her you are here.

NERISSA. There is no need. I'll take you to her room, Lorenzo. This house is my familiar ground.

BALTHASAR. I do not think my lady! . . .

NERISSA. Tush, Balthasar, you are far too formal! Come, Lorenzo, I have something to say to you about your wife.

LORENZO. My wife! Jessica?

NERISSA. I've heard Bassanio's roving eye has lit on her! . . .

LORENZO. Nerissa!

NERISSA. Come! I'll tell you more!

[*They go out together,* LORENZO *expostulating.*

ANTONIO (*to* BALTHASAR). Did you tell your mistress I was here?

BALTHASAR. I did not, my lord.

ANTONIO. Then you are a fool, and do not know your office.

BALTHASAR. A fool, my lord?

ANTONIO. An ass! A jackass! . . .

BALTHASAR. My lord!

[*Enter* LAUNCELOT GOBBO, *from the courtyard in a furtive manner.* GOBBO *has grown slyer in his ways and is a little less certain of himself than he was ten years ago, but he is still something of an amusing rogue.*]

ANTONIO (*to* BALTHASAR). Go now, and tell her I am here.

BALTHASAR. One moment, sir. (*To* GOBBO.) Well, fellow, what is your business?

GOBBO. I wish to see lord Bassanio.

BALTHASAR. He is not at home.

GOBBO. Will it be long before he returns?

BALTHASAR. I do not know.

GOBBO. Then I'll wait. My business is important.

BALTHASAR. As you please. (*To* ANTONIO.) I will acquaint my lady with your presence, sir. (*He mounts the short flight of steps. Then he turns and speaks to* GOBBO.) Your master, Lorenzo, is here.

GOBBO (*dismayed*). My master! . . .

BALTHASAR. I will tell him you are waiting.

GOBBO. No, no, Balthasar, I pray you. My matter is not for his ears.

BALTHASAR. Oh! For whose ears may it be?

GOBBO (*slyly*). Your master's.

BALTHASAR (*understandingly*). I see. Very well! (*Exit.*)

GOBBO (*aside*). That's a pompous ass. He eats starch for dinner and dreams of ramrods.

ANTONIO. Here, fellow!

GOBBO. Sir!

ANTONIO. You are a Venetian?

GOBBO. I am, and you know me well, sir, though your memory is defective. My name is Gobbo, Launcelot Gobbo. I was servant in Venice to Shylock that took a liking to your worship's flesh! . . .

ANTONIO. Servant to Shylock, were you?

GOBBO. And afterwards to my lord Bassanio here, and would be servant to him still, but that my lady could not bear the sight of me. Now I serve Lorenzo that married the Jew's daughter, Jessica.

ANTONIO. I thought I knew your face, but could not remember where I had seen you. Have you ever been in prison?

GOBBO. No, sir, not yet.

ANTONIO. Then you are lucky. But be warned, your luck will not last for ever. You have a most villainous appearance, and on your face alone are certain to be hanged.

GOBBO. Do you wish to say anything more to me, sir?

ANTONIO. Yes. Do you know what day this is?

GOBBO. I am not rightly certain, sir. I slept the clock round on Saturday, and have not yet caught up with time, but some say 'tis Wednesday, though I would not swear to it.

ANTONIO. They all say 'tis Wednesday, as if it were any Wednesday. Why, fellow, 'twas this day, ten years ago, my life was sought by that Jew you served in Venice, that moneylender, Shylock.

GOBBO. Was it, sir?

ANTONIO. But no one remembers, except myself.

GOBBO. We should have remembered the day better, sir, if the Jew had got your flesh. 'Twas always the way of men, sir, to remember successful villainy longer than successful virtue. Here comes my lord Bassanio, and Gratiano with him.

[*Enter* BASSANIO *from the courtyard, followed by* GRATIANO. BASSANIO *is stouter and coarser and more assured in his manner than he was when he came wooing* PORTIA. GRATIANO *has not got so much assurance as* BASSANIO, *but he resembles him otherwise.*]

BASSANIO. Why, here's old Antonio!

ANTONIO. My dear Bassanio! And you, Gratiano!

BASSANIO. What brings you here?

ANTONIO. The hope of seeing you. I am always glad to see you, Bassanio.

GOBBO (*plucking at* BASSANIO'S *sleeve*). My lord!

ANTONIO. Remembering what took place ten years ago this very day, I resolved that I would come and celebrate its memory with you and Portia.

BASSANIO. Oh! And what took place ten years ago?

ANTONIO. What took place! Merciful Father! . . .

BASSANIO. I know! Portia and I were wed!

GRATIANO. And so were Nerissa and I. But is that a cause for celebration, Antonio?

ANTONIO. No, no, I am not talking of your wedding-day, but the day of my deliverance from the Jew.

BASSANIO. Oh, that! Do you hear, Gratiano, it is ten years ago since poor old Antonio nearly lost his pound of flesh.

GRATIANO. I did not think it was so long, and yet sometimes it seems longer.

ANTONIO. I thought the Duke of Venice would have sent a friendly word to me, but no, no one remembers! And when I come here to celebrate the day, I find the house prepared to greet another guest.

BASSANIO. Another guest!

ANTONIO. Yes. Doctor Bellario!

BASSANIO. Doctor Bellario! By heaven, I had forgotten him. Is he here yet?

ANTONIO. No, not yet.

GRATIANO. No, indeed, you don't. I go of my own free will. I thank God I have a mind and can make it up.

NERISSA. Well, then, my lord, make up your mind to this. I like not loneliness. Where have you been these five days and nights ?

GRATIANO. Can a man not go hunting without having to tell his wife all he does ? There's a plague of tiresome women that will have a man detail his life for them, with a " What did you say to him ? " and " What did he say to you ? " and " Where were you at such an hour ? " as if he had memory of all he did. Bassanio and I went hunting. That's enough for you !

NERISSA. Hunting what ?

GRATIANO. Hunting, my dear, just hunting !

PORTIA. Bassanio, I have not asked you much of late, but now I must beg you to curb your pleasure. It has cost me dear, and my fortune will not bear much more. My cousin will confer with me on how to meet our debts.

BASSANIO. So that is why your cousin comes ! It is no friendly visit, but an inquisition. Had I known this, I should have taken my time in hurrying home to greet him.

PORTIA. When he arrives, Bassanio, if you are not here to welcome him, my pardon will be hard to find. Balthasar, are all the invitations sent ?

BALTHASAR. They are, my gracious lady.

[*While* PORTIA *is talking to* BALTHASAR, GOBBO *sidles from his hiding-place and speaks to* BASSANIO.]

PORTIA. There must be many coloured lights when my cousin comes ! And music !

BALTHASAR. It shall be as you wish, my lady. At what hour does Dr. Bellario arrive ?

PORTIA. Soon after dark. Why is Gobbo here ?

BALTHASAR. I do not know, my lady. He brought a message for my lord.

PORTIA. From whom ?

BALTHASAR. He did not say.

PORTIA. Bid him begone.

[BALTHASAR *leaves her and is seen speaking to* GOBBO, *whom he compels to leave the room.* GOBBO *goes into the courtyard, where he conceals himself.*]

PORTIA. Let us go in. All of you will dine to-night

with my cousin and us. Balthasar, while we are within,
bid the servants light the lamps. I wish the house to
look gay when Doctor Bellario arrives.

BALTHASAR. As you please, my lady.

[*Exit* BALTHASAR.

PORTIA. Antonio!

ANTONIO. I come, my dear.

PORTIA. You'll follow me, Nerissa, with my husband
and your lord.

[*She goes into the house with* ANTONIO.

GRATIANO. Now, look here, Nerissa, understand once
and for all, that I will not have you wagging your tongue
about me to Portia.

NERISSA. I'll wag it as I please, and to whom I please.

BASSANIO. If I were your lord, you'd wag it circum-
spectly, madam.

NERISSA. If I were your wife, Bassanio, I'd wag it to
some purpose.

BASSANIO. What do you mean?

NERISSA (*half-way up the steps*). Ask the little Jewess,
Jessica.

BASSANIO. Hell, woman! . . . (*But she has flown.*)
Gratiano, you must make her hold her tongue.

GRATIANO. I will, if you will tell me how!

BASSANIO. Let's follow them.

[GOBBO *returns.*

GOBBO. My lord!

BASSANIO. What! (*Then, seeing who it is.*) Go before
me, Gratiano, and say I'll follow in a little while.

GRATIANO. I'll make a good excuse for you. (*Exit.*)

BASSANIO. What is it, Gobbo?

GOBBO. I have a message for you from my mistress.

BASSANIO. What is it?

GOBBO. She bade me say that my lord Lorenzo's gone
to France. She is alone.

BASSANIO. Oh!

GOBBO. If you will please to come to her! . . .

BASSANIO. Tell her I cannot come. My lady's cousin,
Doctor Bellario, arrives to-night, and I must stay to
welcome him.

GOBBO. My mistress is alone, my lord.

for God knows you are unlikely to cause confusion among the holy angels.

BALTHASAR. Begone! My mistress comes.

[*Exit* GOBBO. *Enter* PORTIA.

PORTIA. Where is your lord, Balthasar?

BALTHASAR. He bade me tell you, my lady, that he had gone to meet your cousin, Doctor Bellario.

PORTIA. Gone to meet my cousin! Are you sure he said that?

BALTHASAR. I am, my lady. His words precisely were " If your mistress should inquire for me, tell her I have gone along the road to meet her cousin, Doctor Bellario." I noted them in my mind at the time.

PORTIA. I am very glad. Was not that Launcelot Gobbo who stole away just now?

BALTHASAR. It was, my lady! A low, ribald fellow, my lady, full of envy and evil wishes. (*He turns to go.*)

PORTIA. One moment, Balthasar!

BALTHASAR. My lady!

PORTIA. This Gobbo, whose servant is he now?

BALTHASAR. I am not well acquainted with the lives of the lower servants, my lady, but I have heard he serves with lord Lorenzo.

PORTIA. Lorenzo!

BALTHASAR. He once was servant, so 'tis said, to lord Lorenzo's father, the Jew of Venice.

PORTIA. Yes! How brightly you have lit the house, Balthasar!

BALTHASAR. My lady, in all I do, I strive to be worthy of your commendation. May I withdraw?

PORTIA. Send Stephano to me.

BALTHASAR. He's by, my lady. I'll summon him. (*He goes to the entrance to the courtyard and calls.*) Stephano!

STEPHANO (*off*). Hola! Hola!

BALTHASAR. He comes, my lady!

PORTIA. Do you like music, Balthasar?

BALTHASAR. I can listen to it, my lady.

PORTIA. Young lord Lorenzo loves music. I remember when he first came here with Jessica, his bride! . . . Jessica! . . .

BALTHASAR. Yes, my lady!

PORTIA (*rousing herself*). I was dreaming, Balthasar, of young times long ago. But not so long ago, not so long in years as long in thought. Lord Lorenzo would sing and play to Jessica ! . . . How I think on Jessica to-night !
[*Enter* STEPHANO.

BALTHASAR. Stephano is here, my lady.

PORTIA. Ah, Stephano !

STEPHANO. My lady !

PORTIA. Sing that song to me which I taught you for the festival. Balthasar, you must stay and hear it, too.

BALTHASAR. My lady, I am no musician.

PORTIA. Nevertheless, I wish you to hear my song. Sing, Stephano.

STEPHANO *sings.*

Come, master youth, count up your charity,
If that your love be not all you desire.
Have you not heard that perfection's a rarity ?
Wedding, like wooing, 's a flickering fire.
    Then droop not,
    Then stoop not,
    Never repine,
Love's a dream that won't come true,
Take what life shall bring to you,
    And make it do.

[*As the song ends, a violent knocking is heard on the gate
  in the courtyard.*]

PORTIA. What noise is that ?

BALTHASAR. Someone knocks on the gate, my lady ! I will see who it is.

[BALTHASAR *goes into the courtyard and opens the gate.
  He speaks to the messenger whom he finds there.*]

PORTIA. You have sung well, Stephano, and I will reward you.

STEPHANO. Shall I continue, my lady?

PORTIA. Not now, Stephano !
[BALTHASAR *returns.*

BALTHASAR. My lady, a messenger has come from Doctor Bellario.

PORTIA. From Doctor Bellario ! Bid him enter.

[BALTHASAR *beckons to the messenger, who enters and
  kneels before* PORTIA.]

women very much, but I do not permit myself to be excessive about them.

STEPHANO. I would love to feel a fierce and uncontrollable passion for a woman.

BALTHASAR. My advice to any young man is this : Be temperate in all things, but especially in love. When you press a woman to your heart, Stephano, do so discreetly and in a moderate manner, so that she may know you are still capable of resisting her. Your father, God rest his soul, was an immoderate man. With what result ? He is a corpse and you are an orphan.

STEPHANO. But do not moderate men die also, master Balthasar ?

BALTHASAR. They do, but not so precipitately.

[*Enter a* SERVANT *in haste.*

BALTHASAR. How now, rascal?

SERVANT. Oh, master Balthasar, the guest is come.

BALTHASAR. Already !

SERVANT. He is almost at the gate.

BALTHASAR. Summon all the servants to the courtyard to bid him welcome. Stir, stir ! (*The* SERVANT *goes out.*) Go, Stephano, and tell my lady her cousin has arrived.

[*Exit* STEPHANO. SERVANTS *appear in the courtyard, which becomes once more full of activity.*]

Be busy, louts and rascals, and when the learned lawyer comes, cheer as if you were glad to see him. (*He goes towards the gates, which have been opened wide by the servants.*) Welcome, welcome, good Doctor Bellario ! . . .

[PORTIA'S *servants make loud sounds of welcome, and some of* BELLARIO'S *servants enter, carrying torches, and are greeted noisily. A trumpet sounds.* PORTIA, *very beautifully dressed, enters from the house and goes to the opening on to the outer courtyard. The hubbub increases in volume. There is music and singing and a great display of coloured lights and torches. Then a passage is made in the crowd, and* DOCTOR BELLARIO *appears. He is an elderly, cynical-looking man.* PORTIA *goes to greet him. He takes her in his arms and kisses her affectionately. Then they both come into the house from the courtyard.*]

PORTIA. My dear cousin, I am glad to bid you welcome again to my house.

BELLARIO. You are not more glad to see me here, Portia, than I am to come. I love this house and often came to it while your father was alive! . . .

PORTIA. It is a grief to me that you have not been here since my marriage.

BELLARIO. Well, well, we'll say no more of that. I lost heavily in reputation through your act, my dear, but we'll say no more of it.

PORTIA. That's more than kind, cousin.

BELLARIO. The whole world would have known my name through that case, had you not misbehaved.

[*The hubbub in the outer courtyard dies down, and the curtains separating the outer from the inner court-yard are drawn.*]

PORTIA. I am sorry for it, dear cousin!

BELLARIO. Well, well, we'll say no more about it. But when I think of how my judgment in that case would have sealed me with the world's renown, O, Portia, Portia!

PORTIA. I can never recompense you, cousin.

BELLARIO. No, you can't—but we'll say no more about it. Where is your husband?

PORTIA. He went to meet you on the road.

BELLARIO. Then he missed me. Which is odd, for there is only one road.

PORTIA. He will be here presently.

[ANTONIO *enters.*

PORTIA (*taking* ANTONIO *by the hand and leading him to* BELLARIO.) Here is one, dear cousin, of more than common interest to you.

BELLARIO. Is he in trouble with the law?

PORTIA. Not now, but was. This is Antonio.

BELLARIO. Antonio!

ANTONIO. I am the merchant of Venice! . . .

BELLARIO. There are many merchants in Venice, sir.

ANTONIO. But none with my reputation.

PORTIA. Antonio is the merchant whose life was sought in Venice by the Jew.

BELLARIO. Oh, yes, yes, yes! I remember now, of course. My cousin and I were just this moment talking of your case, sir. You were the defendant, were you not?

ANTONIO. I was.

BELLARIO. Yes. Yes, yes! It was on your account I quarrelled with my cousin here. Sir, you recall bitter memories to me.

ANTONIO. I myself have bitter memories, sir. Do you know that Shylock as nearly got a pound of my flesh as makes no difference?

BELLARIO. Portia, every time I look on him, I shall think of the wrong you did me.

PORTIA. I trust not, cousin.

ANTONIO. I begin to believe that I am not really popular! . . .

PORTIA. Oh, my dear Antonio, how can you say so?

ANTONIO. Look how everyone regards me! I'm an old man, but I have enough wit left to see that my friends are not effusive about me.

PORTIA. We love you, dear Antonio! . . .

ANTONIO. You say so, and perhaps *you* do, Portia, but Bassanio, whom I loved like my son, dissembles amazingly well. When I came here an hour ago, and told him that this day ten years I was in danger of my death for him, he scarcely had remembrance of it.

PORTIA. He teased you, Antonio.

ANTONIO. And now your cousin here says the sight of me will fill him with bitter memories. I had best go home.

PORTIA. Nay, you shall not. You'll stay and join our festival. Come, cousin, come within and refresh yourself. You'll find Nerissa, that was my clerk, at dinner here to-night. She'll give you deep instruction in the law. I have arranged a feast for you, and there'll be dancing and a youth who sings. Come, Antonio!

BELLARIO. I shall be glad to rest and refresh myself, for I have travelled far to-day.

PORTIA. Come, Antonio!

ANTONIO. Not now. I'll go to my own house, and in the evening when the feast is on, perhaps I'll come again. I bid you good-evening, Doctor Bellario!

BELLARIO. Good evening, sir, to you. (ANTONIO *goes into the courtyard.*)

PORTIA (*calling after him*). Good evening, then, my dear Antonio, but come again to-night.

ANTONIO. I'll think on it, Portia. (*Exit.*)

BELLARIO. That old gentleman is tedious. He is like all litigants. He harps too much on one note.

PORTIA. That is a common way of playing, cousin. I've heard many harp that way.

BELLARIO. True. We all do it. Even I, who am a well-balanced man, sometimes repeat myself.

PORTIA. I am sorry for Antonio. He has nothing in his mind now but his faded reputation, and he does not bear diminishment with dignity. Which of us does? When I am as old as old Antonio, I shall probably find the young impatient with my tales of vanished greatness.

BELLARIO. The remedy for that, my dear Portia, is not to let your greatness vanish.

PORTIA. But there's an enemy we cannot conquer, cousin, our ancient enemy, the clock.

[*Enter* BALTHASAR *from the courtyard.*

BALTHASAR. My lady!

PORTIA. Yes, Balthasar?

BALTHASAR. There is an old man, richly dressed, who's fainted by your gate.

PORTIA. Is it Antonio? He left us a moment since.

BALTHASAR. No, my lady, I do not know this man. He must be a great person in his own country, for I think he is a foreigner.

PORTIA. Bring him in.

[BALTHASAR *goes out.*

BELLARIO. This is some trick of Antonio's to win sympathy. Old men are cunning at such tricks.

PORTIA. But Balthasar says it is not Antonio.

[BALTHASAR *pulls the curtains aside, and two* SERVANTS *enter, carrying a richly dressed old man.*]

BALTHASAR. This is the man, my lady!

PORTIA. Do you not know him?

BALTHASAR. I have never seen him before. He is not a man of Belmont.

PORTIA.   Take him to another room and be kind to him. He is old and looks very tired. (*The* SERVANTS *prepare to carry the old man away, but as they do so he stirs and recovers.*) One moment.   He recovers.   Lay him down gently.

SHYLOCK (*for it is he.*)   Give me water!

BALTHASAR.   He desires a drink of water, my lady.

PORTIA.   One of you bring him some wine.

              [BALTHASAR *instructs a servant to do so.*

SHYLOCK.   What place is this?

BALTHASAR.   This is the palace of my lady.   You are in Belmont.

SHYLOCK.   In Belmont.   Yes, I remember now.   Is that your lady?

BALTHASAR.   Madam, he desires to speak to you.

SHYLOCK.   I thank you, madam, for your kindness and hospitality to a stranger.   I fear I have discomposed your house by my unseasonable sickness.

PORTIA.   Rest here awhile, sir, until you are well again.

SHYLOCK.   Thank you!   It was a faintness that overtook me on the road.

PORTIA.   You are welcome, sir, to all my house can give you.

SHYLOCK.   That is great kindness, madam.   (*Peering at her.*)   Have I not seen you in some other place?

PORTIA.   I do not know.   If you come often to Belmont! . . .

SHYLOCK.   I have never been in Belmont before.   Yet I remember to have seen someone like you.

PORTIA.   Where was it that you saw me?

SHYLOCK.   If I could remember that, madam, I could remember you.   What is your name?

PORTIA.   My name is Portia.   Do you know it?

SHYLOCK.   No. I have never heard it before.   But I have seen your face or someone who resembled you.   Have you a brother?

PORTIA.   No, nor sister neither.

SHYLOCK.   It is a fancy.

PORTIA.   My servants will conduct you to a room where you may rest and recover.   Balthasar!

BALTHASAR.   Yes, my lady?

      [*He leads* SHYLOCK *towards the steps going into the house.*

PORTIA. What is your name, sir ?

SHYLOCK (*pausing and turning to her*). Shylock !

PORTIA (*startled*). Shylock !

SHYLOCK. Shylock is my name !

BALTHASAR. This way, sir !

    [BALTHASAR *goes out, followed by* SHYLOCK.

BELLARIO. What's his name ?

PORTIA. Shylock !

BELLARIO. Shylock ! Was not that the name of the Jew who sought Antonio's life ?

PORTIA. It was.

BELLARIO. Sola ! sola ! By our lady this will be a feast of fun, indeed !

    [*They go into the house and the curtain falls.*

BASSANIO. But what brings the Duke to Belmont ?

ANTONIO. To honour me, Bassanio. You may forget your duty to your kinsman, but my sovereign duke remembers it for you.

BASSANIO. Antonio, you are mad !

[BALTHASAR *returns.*

BALTHASAR. My lady bids me tell you, sir, that she is preparing for the masque and begs that you will hasten to make ready for it. (*He turns to go.*)

BASSANIO. Balthasar !

BALTHASAR. My lord !

BASSANIO. What stranger's in the house ?

BALTHASAR. Doctor Bellario ! . . .

BASSANIO. He is a kinsman of my lady. What stranger came here to-night ?

BALTHASAR. I do not remember how he's called, my lord, but will inquire.

BASSANIO. Does he come from Venice ?

BALTHASAR. He said so, my lord.

BASSANIO. Is he the Duke ?

BALTHASAR. He was not so described nor, indeed, did he look like one.

ANTONIO. How do you know that never saw a duke ? Dukes, God forgive me, are but men in looks, and he's a man, this stranger here, and richly dressed, as you yourself did say. " An old man richly dressed and of great means, but a foreigner." Those were your very words.

BASSANIO. Did you say so, Balthasar ?

BALTHASAR. I did, my lord. The words are accurately repeated, and they describe him accurately.

BASSANIO. Then go and inquire his name. (*Exit* BALTHASAR.) I beg your pardon, Antonio, if I wounded you with my ungraciousness a moment since.

ANTONIO. It is no matter, Bassanio. Old men must learn to bear their juniors' rudeness with what fortitude they can.

BASSANIO. Were you here when Doctor Bellario came ?

ANTONIO. I was. He was scarcely civil to me, but blamed me for his quarrel with Portia. He said the sight of me would fill his mind with bitter memories.

BASSANIO. An ungracious gentleman, then ?

ANTONIO. Very.

BASSANIO. Did Portia speak to him of me ?

ANTONIO. I did not hear her speak of you. I was listening to what was said of me.

[A loud knocking is heard on the outer gate.

BASSANIO. Here come more of our guests, and I am still unready to receive them.

ANTONIO. Wait yet, until Balthasar comes. You are young and can change your dress while older people think about it.

[A SERVANT holds back the curtains, while NERISSA and GRATIANO enter.]

BASSANIO. Ah, here are Nerissa and Gratiano in good time.

NERISSA. Portia bade me to be here before her other guests arrived.

BASSANIO. You'll find her in her chamber making ready for a masque.

GRATIANO. Good ! I glory in masques !

NERISSA. It is most unseemly at your age to be a masquer or to take so much delight in anything. You should be more sober and think about your grave.

GRATIANO. I am not likely to forget it while you're about.

NERISSA. I wish you would remember to be faithful, then.

GRATIANO. There you go. Fidelity ! Always fidelity ! But what is fidelity ? Lack of imagination ! . . .

NERISSA. You'd better not let Portia hear you speaking so. She has little use for flippant talk.

BASSANIO. Come, come, Nerissa. Join Portia in her room.

NERISSA (*mounting the steps*). There'll be an ill end to all this amorous adventuring, master Gratiano. Mark my words for that ! If men may philander, then women will philander, too, and the end of that is hard to see.

GRATIANO (*kissing his hand to her*). God's blessing on your cheery talk, my sweet wife ! (NERISSA *angrily goes out.*) Her conversation is a continual tale of calamity. I wish her no harm, but if God should see fit to call her hence, I should not resent it.

BASSANIO. There is an old, rich man from Venice here who is, so Antonio says, the Duke.

GRATIANO. The Duke of Venice!

[*Re-enter* BALTHASAR.

BASSANIO. So Antonio says. Well, Balthasar, what is the stranger's name?

BALTHASAR. Shylock, my lord!

GRATIANO. ⎫ Shylock!
BASSANIO. ⎭

ANTONIO. Did you say " Shylock "?

BALTHASAR. That is the stranger's name. I said it was a foreign one, not easy to remember.

BASSANIO. Shylock! . . . You're mad, you pompous fool, to say that Shylock's here!

BALTHASAR. Mad, my lord! Me, mad! No, my lord!

BASSANIO. Who told you this?

BALTHASAR. My lady's maid. I bade her ask my mistress for the stranger's name that I might repeat it to you.

BASSANIO. This is one of Portia's jests. She has a strange sense of humour.

BALTHASAR. She did not seem to jest, my lord. The stranger's come to see his daughter here—Lord Lorenzo's lady!

BASSANIO. Lorenzo's lady! ,

GRATIANO. Jessica!

ANTONIO. The Jew's daughter!

BASSANIO (*to* BALTHASAR). Where is this man, Shylock?

BALTHASAR. Resting within, my lord.

BASSANIO. Bid him come here.

BALTHASAR. He is not well, my lord.

BASSANIO. Bid him come here, I tell you.

[BALTHASAR *goes in.*

ANTONIO. And I believed he was the Duke.

GRATIANO. Come to do you honour, Antonio! Perhaps he's come to have another look at your flesh.

BASSANIO. Why did Portia let him in?

GRATIANO. Perhaps she did not know it was the Jew. She saw him only once—that day Antonio was tried in Venice.

BASSANIO. Did Bellario bring him here?

ANTONIO. They did not come together. I saw the Doctor arrive.

[*Enter* LAUNCELOT GOBBO *through the curtains.*

GOBBO. My lord Bassanio!

BASSANIO. What is it now, fool?

GOBBO. My mistress bade me tell you she has changed her mind.

BASSANIO. Go back and tell her I have changed mine, too!

GOBBO. She weeps, my lord.

BASSANIO. Let her weep.

GOBBO. And repents that she used you ill.

BASSANIO. Does she admit that she used me ill?

GOBBO. Yes, my lord, and she bids you come to her again.

BASSANIO. She knows I cannot come to her now. I told her why.

GOBBO (*confidentially*). My lord, she will receive you in her room after the feast is finished. My lady, your wife, has bid her here to dinner. It might be she and you could steal away together. She bade me say so.

BASSANIO. She is a fool to trust you thus, Gobbo, but if ever you betray her to her lord, I'll have the heart out of you.

[SHYLOCK *enters, followed by* BALTHASAR.

GOBBO. I will remember, my lord. (*Sees* SHYLOCK.) Oh, God, the Jew!

SHYLOCK. Gobbo! Launcelot Gobbo! (*Looks round at the company.*) Antonio!

BASSANIO. You are Shylock!

SHYLOCK. And you are Bassanio?

BASSANIO. That is my name.

SHYLOCK (*to* GRATIANO). And you?

GRATIANO. My name is Gratiano.

SHYLOCK. Bassanio's friend. I had forgotten your face. It is a face one might forget. What house is this?

BASSANIO. My house.

SHYLOCK. Your house? I thought it was the house of Portia.

BASSANIO. The lady Portia is my wife.

SHYLOCK. That noble lady is your wife?

BASSANIO. I am her husband and father to her children.

SHYLOCK. I did not know. (*To* GOBBO.) Where is my daughter ?

GOBBO. Oh, master Jew, close by ! I'll tell her you are here.

SHYLOCK. Go quickly. I am not well ! . . . (*He sways and would fall were not* BALTHASAR *by to catch him.*)

GOBBO. I'll go at once. Oh, God, the Jew ! (*Exit.*)

ANTONIO. Bid him begone, Bassanio. You cannot have him here.

SHYLOCK. Bear me to my room again, Balthasar. I am not well, and this meeting has not made me better.

BASSANIO. One moment, Jew. I do not wish you to stay here.

SHYLOCK. When morning comes, I'll go.

BASSANIO. I'd have you go to-night.

SHYLOCK. To-night ?

BASSANIO. Now.

SHYLOCK. It is late, but I will go if you will give me time to rest myself. My daughter's house is near ! . . .

GRATIANO. How, Jew, comes it that you wear these gaudy clothes ?

BASSANIO. Yes. Where is your gaberdine, damned Jew ?

SHYLOCK (*now recovered from his first distress*). I am not a damned Jew. I am a damned Christian.

BASSANIO. What's this ?

GRATIANO. A Christian ! You ?

SHYLOCK. I am a Christian.

GRATIANO. By conviction ?

SHYLOCK. No, sir, by compulsion. I was converted, you'll remember, in the Court at Venice. Antonio here was my godfather.

ANTONIO. I ? Godfathered you !

SHYLOCK. You did ! You did, my dear Antonio, and rendered me great service in doing it, for all my legal disabilities were removed when you insisted on my christening. I am a citizen of Venice now, and not an alien Jew any more. I'm free to go and come as I please and wear what garments take my fancy. And I am rich again and favoured by the Duke, to whom I have done much service. I thank you, Antonio, for all you did for me.

ANTONIO. God's grace, man, thank not me.

SHYLOCK. I must, Antonio, I must, since all I have I owe to you. Many a time and oft, when I have added richly to my store of wealth or had additions to the honours paid me by the Duke, I've thought of you and thanked you heartily, Antonio.

GRATIANO. Does the Duke honour you ?

ANTONIO. That never honoured me ?

SHYLOCK. I am now a member of the Senate.

ANTONIO. You, a Senator !

SHYLOCK. I thank you for it, good Antonio. It's strange that I should meet you here so soon, for when I told the Duke seven days ago that I was venturing forth from Venice and wondered if I'd meet you here in Belmont, he did not well remember you—he's growing old, so you must pardon him—but I recalled you to his memory, whereon he spoke of you.

ANTONIO. What did he say ?

SHYLOCK. He said—I have his very words—" I remember now. A tiresome gentleman who preached ! "

ANTONIO. Preached !

SHYLOCK. No, I'm wrong. The word was " moralized." Moralized ! That was the word. " A tiresome gentleman who moralized ! "

ANTONIO. 'Tis false. I'm not a moralizer.

BASSANIO. Enough of this ! Honoured or not honoured, you're still a Jew to me, Shylock. If you were God Himself, I'd call you Jew, and bid you leave my house.

SHYLOCK. I am not God Himself, that's sure, but if I were, you would do well to call me Jew ! . . .

GRATIANO. This is blasphemy !

BASSANIO. I'll have no quibbling here. Go !

SHYLOCK. I'll go, my lord. My presence cannot give you less pleasure than yours gives me.

BASSANIO. Be careful with your tongue, Jew.

SHYLOCK. Were I less careful with my tongue, Bassanio, than you were with your friends, I'd long ago have hanged.

BASSANIO. What's your meaning now ?

SHYLOCK. Ask your kinsman here, Antonio, who lent

you money ne'er repaid, and was forgot the moment it
was lent. Is that not so, Antonio?

ANTONIO. That's no affair of yours, Jew.

SHYLOCK. No? Three thousand ducats that were
mine were lent to him on your security. I never had it
back. Your life was mine. I did not get that either.
But Bassanio had as little thought for your life as he had
for my ducats. There is a sin, Bassanio, that stretches
far beyond most sins, ingratitude, and you are deeply
practised in it.

BASSANIO. Be silent, cur!

SHYLOCK. I am a citizen of Venice and entitled to
civility from you, my lord.

BASSANIO. There's no civility for you nor any Jew.
Your race is outlawed from the world's compassion.
There is not, nor ever will be, peace 'twixt us and you.
You are a Jew.

SHYLOCK. I am a Jew! . . .

GRATIANO. Turned Christian!

SHYLOCK. Turned Christian by compulsion. I had no
choice in this, whether to be a Jew or a Christian, even
as you, Gratiano, had no choice in your birth. You are
a Christian for the reason I'm a Jew, that you were born
so. Had you been born, as I was born, a Jew! . . .

GRATIANO. That could never have been. A Turk,
perhaps, and there is much that is commendable in Turks,
but a Jew, no! Never! I should have foresworn birth
rather than be born a Jew.

SHYLOCK. We are not masters of our birth, Gratiano.
God does not stop to ask us what our nationality
shall be.

GRATIANO. God is wise and makes the best of His
material. That which He loves, He makes into Christians.
That which He dislikes, He makes into Jews.

BASSANIO. Let's have no more argument. Come, Jew,
make ready to go!

SHYLOCK. I have not done, my lord. I meant to say
that though I am a Jew, I would not in my most extremity
have left my friend as you left Antonio. You are a pretty
gentleman, my lord Bassanio, to deck yourself with bought
nobility that came to Belmont here to hunt a fortune

with borrowed means, and left your friend to pay your debt, if need be, with his life.

BASSANIO. By God I'll bear no more of this.

SHYLOCK. I am a Jew, you say, and you a Christian. I wish your Saviour joy of you!

BASSANIO. Out, I tell you, lest I throw you to my dogs.

[PORTIA, *in her richest dress, enters.*

PORTIA. My lord! What noise is this?

BASSANIO. This man—do you know him?

PORTIA. I do. He is Shylock.

ANTONIO. That tried to take my life.

PORTIA. Yes, but failed, Antonio. Come, Shylock, you should not be here in this cold air. Balthasar, bear him back to his chamber.

BASSANIO. Madam, I have commanded him to leave this house to-night.

PORTIA. And why, my lord?

BASSANIO. Because it is my will.

PORTIA. But I, my lord, will otherwise. Come, Shylock!

ANTONIO. How can you keep him here when I am by?

PORTIA. Are you a reason why I should be uncivil to an old man, sick at my gate? . . .

BASSANIO. But this is Shylock, the Jew!

PORTIA. Well? We had our quarrel with him, which we won. Are we to keep it up forever?

ANTONIO. I can keep it up, and will!

PORTIA. I am ashamed of you, Antonio, to be so rancorous, and you so near the grave. I tremble for you on the Judgment Day.

BASSANIO. I tell you yet again, Portia, I will not tolerate this Jew! . . .

SHYLOCK. I pray you, madam, give me leave to go from hence.

PORTIA. No. You are not well. The hour is late. You'll stay until the morning.

BASSANIO. Madam!

PORTIA. My lord!

BASSANIO. Be warned! Think well of what you say and what you do!

PORTIA. I have thought well, Bassanio!

BASSANIO. If he remains within this house to-night, I will not stay with you.

SHYLOCK. Madam! . . .

PORTIA. Your presence, my lord, has not been so comforting that I am likely to mourn your absence. My cousin, Doctor Bellario, will speak to you about the money you have wasted.

[*Enter* JESSICA *from the outer court. She is very beautiful, but is still the mean little sweep she was when she ran away with* LORENZO. *Her beauty is slightly marred by lines of discontent about her eyes and mouth, and she is more obviously sensual than she was ten years ago. She goes to* BASSANIO.]

JESSICA. What tale is this I hear from Gobbo? . . . Oh, God, my father!

SHYLOCK (*profoundly moved by the sight of her*). Jessica! My little Jessica!

JESSICA. Why did you come here?

SHYLOCK. I came in search of you, but sickened at this lady's gate.

PORTIA. I have received your father as my guest, Jessica, and wish that he will stay with us 'til he is well again.

JESSICA. But that's impossible, Portia. Father, you must go back to Venice.

SHYLOCK. Why? Will you not receive me?

JESSICA. I cannot, father. Lorenzo does not love you.

SHYLOCK. Do you love me?

JESSICA. You are my father.

SHYLOCK. Do *you* love me?

JESSICA. Your house was hard! . . .

SHYLOCK. I loved you, Jessica, as no man ever loved his child, and I dreamt great dreams for you, but you destroyed them.

JESSICA. You were too hard, father. I could not love you.

SHYLOCK. Ungrateful girl, well were you wed to a Christian gentleman. You fled from me that loved you, and stole my money to endow a man that daily made a mock of me and my religion. And since that day I've heard no word from you, nor have you ever questioned was I alive or dead.

JESSICA. I did not love you, father. I cannot love by rule, but as I'm swayed.

SHYLOCK. So. Did you love your mother, Jessica?

JESSICA. I do not well remember her.

SHYLOCK. When Tubal, my friend, came to me in Venice after you had fled and told me of your wasteful wanderings, there was one thing you did that tore my heart in pieces.

JESSICA. I do not now remember what I did. 'Tis very long ago.

SHYLOCK. I have not forgotten, nor will I ever forget. I'll tell you, girl, what it was that killed me here. (*Touching his breast.*)

BASSANIO. Well, tell her somewhere else.

PORTIA. My lord, you're strangely lacking in civility.

SHYLOCK (*to* PORTIA). I will not trespass on your hospitality too long, my lady. (*To* JESSICA.) Your mother, while I was still a bachelor, gave me a ring, a turquoise ring, the first of all the gifts I had from her, and I valued it, and loved it more than all I had. You stole it from me, Jessica, the night you fled from Venice with your lover, lord Lorenzo.

JESSICA. I'll look for it and give it back to you again.

SHYLOCK. You will not find it nor can you ever give it back to me. So little value had your mother's ring for you, Jessica, though it was very dear to me, that you sold it for a monkey there in Genoa. O, God of Israel, how that hurt my heart!

JESSICA. I did not think. I pray you, father, return to Venice now.

SHYLOCK. I've heard that you have children. How many?

JESSICA. Three, father. Three sons!

SHYLOCK. Three sons! You have been blessed, Jessica. How are they named?

JESSICA. The first is called Lorenzo, for his father! . . .

SHYLOCK. His father! Yes?

JESSICA. The second! . . .

SHYLOCK. The second, yes! Yes, the second?

JESSICA. Is called for his godfather here, Antonio.

SHYLOCK. Antonio! I see! Godfathering's a general

habit with you, Antonio. First the grandsire and then the grandson. Well? How is the third named?

JESSICA. After my lord Bassanio.

SHYLOCK. Your lord Bassanio! Did you forget my name?

JESSICA. My husband does not like Jews.

SHYLOCK. Yet he loves you?

JESSICA. I am a woman.

SHYLOCK. Have your children ever heard of me, their grandsire?

JESSICA. We do not speak of you, father.

SHYLOCK. Do they like Jews?

GRATIANO. I'll answer you for that, old Shylock. I heard the littlest one, that's called after you, Bassanio, cry as he strided up and down the passage to Lorenzo's house, " Down with the Jews! Down with the dirty Jews! "

SHYLOCK (*after a moment's silence*). Yet they are Jews.

GRATIANO. How now, Jews?

ANTONIO. I saw them christened at the font for little Christians, and the one that's named after me has a nose the Pope himself might wear.

SHYLOCK. Yet are they Jews, for they have my blood in their little Christian hearts.

GRATIANO. But you said that you were a Christian, too.

SHYLOCK. Do you then acknowledge me to be a Christian?

GRATIANO. I do not know. I am weak on theology. What do you say, Antonio? You godfathered him.

ANTONIO. He is, perhaps, a Christian in law, but not as one born to it. A half-and-half sort of a Christian, with one leg in heaven and t'other in hell!

BASSANIO. I care not where his legs may be so that they be not here. Come, Jew-Christian, Christian-Jew, are you going?

PORTIA. I have already answered that for you, my lord. This gentleman will stay with us to-night.

BASSANIO. Then *I* shall go to-night.

PORTIA. That's as you please, Bassanio!

[*Enter* DOCTOR BELLARIO *from the house.*

PORTIA. Here's my cousin, come in time to greet you before you go. This, Bassanio, is Doctor Bellario.

BELLARIO. It seems I missed you on the road.

BASSANIO. Missed me ?

BELLARIO. You went to meet me, so your servant said.

BASSANIO. True ! I somehow lost my way in the dark.

BELLARIO. You have not yet learned your way about Belmont ?

BASSANIO. I know it very well.

BELLARIO. Ha !

BASSANIO. I'm glad to meet you, sir, and welcome you to Belmont. But first, let me rid the house of this pernicious Jew ! . . .

BELLARIO. Who ? Shylock ?

BASSANIO. You know him, then ?

PORTIA. They met an hour or two ago, Bassanio, while you were losing your way.

BELLARIO (*to* SHYLOCK). You were the plaintiff in that suit against Antonio.

SHYLOCK. I was.

BELLARIO. A most interesting case—most interesting, but shockingly handled from your point of view. My dear sir, a man who is his own counsel has a fool for a client. If you had engaged me to plead your case, I think Antonio here would be considerably lighter than he is.

ANTONIO. God's grace, sir !

BELLARIO (*taking hold of* ANTONIO). A pound of flesh ! After all, it isn't much.

ANTONIO. By your leave sir, it's enough !

GRATIANO. Truly, Antonio, for there is scarcely enough meat on your bones to make up to the full of a pound. You are a very lean man.

BELLARIO. Not so lean as he would be if Shylock had had his way. Eh, Antonio ? Ha, ha, ha ! (*Slaps* ANTONIO *on the back without, however, provoking any mirth from* ANTONIO.) I wish you'd engaged me, Shylock. I'd have won your case for you.

ANTONIO. By our Lady, this lawyer talks of pounds of a man's flesh as if they were pounds of potatoes.

BELLARIO. I heard you say, Bassanio, you wished to rid the house of a Jew ?

BASSANIO. Yes. This Jew, Shylock !

BELLARIO. But he's a Christian now—legally. You'd

best be careful how you call a Christian a Jew, especially if he is a Jew. He could sue you in the Courts for defamation of character. Shylock, if you bring a suit against him, I hope you'll retain me.

BASSANIO. I like not this sort of banter, sir.

BELLARIO. I guessed as much from gazing on you, my good Bassanio. How comes it that you missed me on the road when there is only one road leads that way?

BASSANIO. I do not know. 'Twas dark.

BELLARIO. But light enough for me to find my way. Your eyes, perhaps, mislead you, Bassanio. You should have them attended to by a surgeon.

[*Enter* BALTHASAR.

BALTHASAR. Madam, the guests assemble.

PORTIA. Bid them enter. Come, Shylock, return to your chamber. You will not wish to see our festival while you are sick and tired.

SHYLOCK. Madam, I have a daughter here. It is to her house I should go.

JESSICA. My husband would not welcome you.

PORTIA. Your husband is not at home, Jessica.

JESSICA. No, Portia, but when he returns! . . .

PORTIA. I understand! There's no place else for you, Shylock, to-night. You must stay here.

SHYLOCK. I am your servant, madam.

PORTIA. Good-night, Shylock.

SHYLOCK. Good-night, Portia. (*He raises her hand to his lips and then goes out.*)

PORTIA (*to* BALTHASAR). Let the guests come in.

BASSANIO. By God, my lady, I'll bear no more of this! . . .

[BALTHASAR *has drawn the curtains, and the guests in rich and gay clothes can be seen crossing the outer courtyard.*]

PORTIA. Our guests assemble, my lord!

BASSANIO. I care not for our guests or you! . . .

[PORTIA *goes forward to meet the guests, who enter in quick succession. There is much animation, and presently the sound of music is heard. The scene gradually fills up.*]

BELLARIO (*aside to* BASSANIO). You'd best be friends

with Shylock, young gentleman. Your fortunes are askew, and he may be willing to lend you money.

BASSANIO.   Lend me money ! . . .

BELLARIO.   S-s-s-sh ! . . . (*He goes to* PORTIA *and mingles with the guests.*)

JESSICA.   Bassanio ! (*No answer.*) Bassanio !

BASSANIO.   What ! Are you still here ?

JESSICA.   Why, yes, Bassanio. I am a guest to-night.

BASSANIO.   Then go and be one.

JESSICA (*reproachfully*).   Bassanio ! Bassanio !

BASSANIO.   What, hussy ?

JESSICA.   I sent a message to you to-night by Gobbo.

BASSANIO.   I got it, I got it !

JESSICA.   But gave no answer to it.

BASSANIO.   There was no answer.

JESSICA.   Oh, Bassanio ! . . .

BASSANIO.   Be quiet, fool ! Someone will hear you !

JESSICA.   Come to me to-night. I'll promise you all you desire.

BASSANIO.   You were not so complaisant when I saw you last.

JESSICA.   I only meant to tease you.

BASSANIO.   Tease me, by God ! I'm not a man that can endure teasing. If you wish to have my love, Jessica, be circumspect and yielding. I have no time for teasing ways.

JESSICA.   I'll do whatever you bid me, Bassanio.

BASSANIO.   This way of wooing women with subtlety and coy advances and delicate retreats—I'm not for that, but for plain, blunt love, and be done with it. I had my enough of teasing ways when I was young, but now I'm for decision, sudden and abrupt. Will you love ? Then love ! Will you not love ? Then go and be damned ! Do you understand me, Jessica ? No dalliance, no whimsy-whamsies, no long entreaties, but swift surrender and unresisting love for me.

JESSICA.   Yes, Bassanio, I understand and will obey you in everything.

BASSANIO.   I like obedient women. I'll come to you to-night. Soon after twelve, we'll steal away together. Do you hear ?

JESSICA. Yes, Bassanio.

> [*There is a movement in the crowd, and* PORTIA *leading* DOCTOR BELLARIO, *comes forward.*]

PORTIA. Dear friends, let us go in. Bassanio, will you bring Jessica ?

> [*She goes out with* DOCTOR BELLARIO, *followed by* BASSANIO *and* JESSICA, *and the rest of the guests. The stage is left empty for a few moments. We still hear the music, and can see the coloured lights in the courtyard.* LAUNCELOT GOBBO *sneaks into the outer yard and then into the inner one. He looks about him, and then goes towards the steps leading into the house. As he does so,* SHYLOCK *appears at the head of them.* GOBBO *gives a gulp of alarm.*]

SHYLOCK. Gobbo !

GOBBO. Sir !

SHYLOCK (*descending the steps*). You serve my daughter and her husband, do you not ?

GOBBO. Yes, sir, I do, sir. Truly I do.

SHYLOCK. Is their house far from here ?

GOBBO. A goodly step, sir.

SHYLOCK. Will you take me to it ?

GOBBO. But my lady, your daughter, she is here, at the festival !

SHYLOCK. I know. Gobbo, I would like to see my grandsons. Will you not gratify my wish ?

GOBBO. But, sir, if my mistress will not ! . . .

SHYLOCK. I will pay you well, Gobbo, and no one need know. They'll be asleep now, will they not ?

GOBBO. I hope so, sir.

SHYLOCK. Then gratify me this much, and I'll reward you well.

GOBBO. But I cannot come on the instant, sir. My lady bade me wait for her here. She has instructions for me.

SHYLOCK. How long are you to wait ?

GOBBO. Until she sends for me. Women are sometimes dilatory, sir.

SHYLOCK. This festival will last the night ?

GOBBO. It will, sir, though some will not last with it.

SHYLOCK. When you have had my daughter's message, send for me and take me to her house! . . .

GOBBO. I dare not, sir.

SHYLOCK. I'll pay you well, Gobbo, and none shall know I've seen my grandsons but yourself and me. I'll look at them and come away again. You'll gratify me? (GOBBO *hesitates.* SHYLOCK *produces a purse and clinks the money in it.*) Well, Gobbo?

GOBBO. I will, sir. After all, it is a Christian act to let a grandsire see his grandsons.

SHYLOCK. Even though he be a Jew. Go, Gobbo, and get your message, and come again for me.

[GOBBO *goes in, and* SHYLOCK *is left in the dusk, listening to the music.*]

THE THIRD ACT

[*The scene is a pillared hall in* PORTIA'S *house. When the curtain ascends, the guests are found dancing to lively music.* PORTIA *and* DOCTOR BELLARIO *are dancing together.* BASSANIO *is dancing with* JESSICA. GRATIANO *is dancing with a young and pretty girl.* NERISSA *is sitting with* ANTONIO, *to whom, however, she pays very little attention, for she is jealously watching her husband and his partner.*]

ANTONIO. I am uncomfortable, Nerissa, when I remember that that Jew is here, a room or two away from me. I do not like the thought, and I take it very ill from Portia that she keeps him here.

NERISSA. Do you see that girl with Gratiano?

ANTONIO. What girl? Where?

NERISSA. Dancing now with Gratiano. Who is she?

ANTONIO. I do not know, Nerissa, and I was talking of the Jew.

NERISSA. I think her face surpasses all I've ever seen in ugliness.

ANTONIO. Whose face?

NERISSA. Hers—that hussy with the tawny hair who ogles Gratiano with her squinting eyes.

ANTONIO (*peering at the girl*). Does she squint?

NERISSA. Most vilely. And he squints who cannot see that she squints. She is a smirking wench that has no modesty of mind or shape. She'll die in bad repute, if I know anything, and live in it, too.

ANTONIO. Has she done you an injury?

NERISSA. Any woman who interests my husband does me an injury.

ANTONIO. I fear he does not make you happy, Nerissa.

NERISSA. He does not.

ANTONIO. Then why continue in his house ?

NERISSA. Because I love him, fool. Do you remember how my lady won Bassanio ?

ANTONIO. I do, and have good cause to remember it, for that was how the Jew ! . . .

NERISSA. Oh, hold your peace about the Jew !

ANTONIO. Faith, he nearly held a piece of me.

NERISSA. At last, Antonio, you have made a joke. There's hope for you, but Jew me no Jew, I beg. My mistress' father left a will ! . . .

ANTONIO. I remember.

NERISSA. A foolish old man's will that you might leave—whereby her hand was given to him who chose the right one of three caskets.

ANTONIO. Yes. One of gold, one of silver, and one of lead. Who chose the last, won Portia.

NERISSA. So. Her father, being old and mad, God help him, thought by this device to save her from fortune-hunters.

ANTONIO. It was not a successful device.

NERISSA. It was not, for never on this earth was there a fortune-hunter equal to Bassanio. But my lady loved him for his handsome looks and bearing, and I loved Gratiano for the same. How do you think Bassanio chose the right casket ?

ANTONIO. I've heard the story. There's a ballad made of it. By wisdom, I suppose, or good fortune.

NERISSA. By rubbish. He has not enough wit in his head to make a sensible choice of anything. I told him which to choose.

ANTONIO. You told him ! . . .

NERISSA. Portia hinted that I should, and I was nothing loth, for if she had not got him, I should not have had Gratiano.

ANTONIO. What loss would that have been ?

NERISSA. Old man, anything you want but do not get, is a loss, whether it be good or bad. I told Bassanio which casket he must choose, and thus he won Portia.

ANTONIO. And so her father's will was defeated. The

lovely words, with which he wooed and won me. But now he repeats himself.

JESSICA. He speaks in a very gallant and fascinating way to women.

PORTIA. Is that how he speaks to you?

JESSICA. Oh, no! His manner's always courteous to me, but I've been told his syllables are full of charm when he is bent on wooing.

PORTIA. From whom did you hear this?

JESSICA. From Lorenzo and Nerissa and her husband, Gratiano. From you, and all who know him.

PORTIA. He has not told you so himself?

JESSICA. Oh, no! He has respect for you and Lorenzo.

PORTIA. That's new to me. Shall I send your father to you in the morning?

JESSICA. I beg you, no. Bid him go back to Venice.

PORTIA. He's such an old man, Jessica, and gentler now than when he sued Antonio. He has not seen your children, and he would like to see them.

JESSICA. I dare not have him while Lorenzo's gone.

PORTIA. Bassanio's angry with me because I keep your father here, and threatens he will quarrel with me if I let him stay. Will you not take your father home with you to-night that I may keep peace with my husband?

JESSICA. To-night?

PORTIA. Now. I'll send for him. There's nowhere else for him to go.

JESSICA. Oh no, I cannot consent to that. Let him remain with you to-night. I'll think what's best to do to-morrow. Not to-night.

PORTIA. Why, what's to do, Jessica? You shake with apprehension.

JESSICA. I cannot have my father home to-night.

PORTIA. Well, then, we'll leave him here until the morning. Look! The dance begins again. Come, Gratiano, dance with me. Who'll dance with Jessica?

BASSANIO. I will, with all my heart.

BELLARIO. Bassanio, let this dance go by. I've something more to say to you.

BASSANIO. But Jessica! . . .

JESSICA. This gentleman will dance with me.

[*She goes off with a guest. The music begins again
and continues, with dancing, through the next scene.*]

BASSANIO. Your looks are grave, Bellario.

BELLARIO. Yours should be graver! My cousin's
fortune is almost dissipated.

BASSANIO. A man must live and have enjoyment.

BELLARIO. The world would be more comfortable,
Bassanio, if we could make our life and our pleasure equal
in duration with our means. To die when the last coin
is spent and the last pleasure tasted would no doubt be
an excellent end. But Heaven is not always so exact as
that, my cousin, and you are likely to outlast your
means by a long time. There's little left.

BASSANIO. Can we not raise more money?

BELLARIO. On what?

BASSANIO. On anything.

BELLARIO. I fear that your reputation as a debtor,
Bassanio, does you little credit. There's only one way to
keep means and life on some sort of equality.

BASSANIO. And what's that?

BELLARIO. Thrift—inexorable thrift.

BASSANIO. I like it not.

BELLARIO. I was afraid you wouldn't, but, like or not
like, you must intrigue with thrift, Bassanio, if you are
not to lose your wife's estate. You have a pretty gift
for spending what's not your own.

BASSANIO. I do not catch your meaning.

BELLARIO. I remember that you won my cousin's hand
with money that was borrowed, but was not repaid.

BASSANIO. I've heard more than enough about that
money. Antonio has me deafened with his reminders of
it, and now this Jew comes to keep the world in memory
of it. God, but I'd give ten times the sum to have him
out of this.

BELLARIO. You mean that you would get someone else
to give ten times the sum.

BASSANIO. Have it as you will.

BELLARIO. Why are you so anxious to expel him from
your house? A Jew's a harmless, necessary person. Since
we cannot be thrifty for ourselves, we must have Jews to

JESSICA. She spoke oddly to me now, but I swore that I only loved Lorenzo.

BASSANIO. And do you love Lorenzo?

JESSICA. You know that I love you, not him. I cannot bear his moonstruck talk of music. Night after night he reads his verses to me, until I want to scream, but dare not, lest he say I have no soul. Oh, I like rude, rough men, that catch a woman without pity and use her how they will. I hate this soft musician's love that will not hurt me except with phrases.

[*Enter* GRATIANO *and* NERISSA.

GRATIANO. Bassanio!

BASSANIO. Yes, Gratiano.

GRATIANO. I have a scheme! . . .

NERISSA. 'Twas I that thought of it.

GRATIANO. True, she thought of it, but I approved it. It's this. But wait, Jessica is here.

BASSANIO. What odds for that?

GRATIANO. It concerns her father.

BASSANIO. No matter. Go on.

JESSICA. I'll come again when you are done. (*Exit.*)

GRATIANO. It is a scheme to rid you of Shylock and reconcile you to your wife without the loss of dignity to either.

BASSANIO. That will be difficult.

GRATIANO. Not so difficult as you imagine. Shylock does not know who Portia is.

BASSANIO. He knows she is my wife.

GRATIANO. But nothing more. He does not know she is the lawyer that defrauded him of old Antonio's flesh. He saw her once in Venice, in the Duke's Court, and thought she was a man, as indeed, we did ourselves, Bassanio, and has not seen her since until to-day.

NERISSA. Nor does he know I was her clerk. He thought that I, too, was a man.

GRATIANO. I wish you were.

NERISSA. If I were a man, as you're a man, I'd break your skull!

BASSANIO. I pray you, keep this connubial conversation for another time. I have enough of it at home, without importing any.

GRATIANO. The scheme is this. We'll tell Shylock who Portia is, and he'll be so enraged, he'll go at once without a word.

BASSANIO. That scheme's no good. He'll not believe it.

GRATIANO. He will not doubt our word!

NERISSA. He will. I would myself. Some other scheme! . . . (*She goes apart to cogitate.*)

BASSANIO. Time was when women gave obedience to their husbands.

GRATIANO. When was that time?

BASSANIO. I do not know.

GRATIANO. Nor I nor anyone.

BASSANIO. In Eastern lands, they say, women give strict obedience to their lords.

GRATIANO. The East is far away, Bassanio, or I would go to it.

BASSANIO. I'd like to have an Eastern wife—a little, clinging, dark-haired, soft, obedient wife, that came when called and went when told. These tall, blond women claim too much equality with us. I know a little, clinging, dark-haired woman! . . .

GRATIANO. Has she a sister like herself?

BASSANIO. She is content to love when she is bid— a little, servile, unassertive thing! . . .

GRATIANO. What is her name?

BASSANIO. Her name! No matter! . . .

GRATIANO. Is her name Jessica?

BASSANIO. No matter!

GRATIANO. I wish the Jew had gotten twins when he got her.

NERISSA. I have another scheme, a most valiant and noble scheme! . . .

GRATIANO. Say it out, then!

NERISSA. We'll try Antonio a second time.

BASSANIO. Try Antonio! . . .

NERISSA. As he was tried in Venice. We'll persuade Portia that Doctor Bellario would like to see her in her lawyer's robes and hear how she conducted old Antonio's trial.

BASSANIO. Well, what then?

NERISSA. Meanwhile, we'll have the Jew in hiding

here on some pretext, and when he sees her enter in her
robes, he'll recognize her and depart.

BASSANIO. But he may not depart.

NERISSA. He will, for he is full of pride. Besides,
we'll make such game of him in trial that he will not
wish to stay and see it ended. Doctor Bellario can be
the Duke, Antonio, himself! . . .

BASSANIO. Who'll play the Jew?

GRATIANO. Let me. I warrant you I'll make a fierce
and bloody-minded Jew and shrug my shoulders and
spread my hands—O, I'll be a Jew to deceive Moses.

NERISSA. Here comes Portia. Go, Gratiano, and
instruct Antonio in his part, and when we have persuaded
Portia to play, I'll go with her to help her with her robes.
While we are gone, get the Jew here and hide him in a
corner.

GRATIANO. For this, my heart's delight, I'll love you
as I should.

        [*Exit* GRATIANO. *As he goes out,* PORTIA *enters.*

PORTIA. Where's Gratiano going?

NERISSA. To find Antonio. We have a plan to entertain your cousin, Portia.

PORTIA. I've come to find him. Our guests are in the
garden, watching a masque. Will you not come and see
it, Nerissa?

NERISSA. Presently I will, but now! . . .

PORTIA. Bassanio, we should be with our guests.

NERISSA. Bassanio has confessed to me, Portia, his
grief that you and he have quarrelled. He wishes to be
friends with you again.

PORTIA. Do you, Bassanio?

NERISSA. See how his tongue misgives him. He cannot
speak, because he feels so much. Come, Portia, come,
Bassanio, be friends.

PORTIA. With all my heart, Bassanio, I will be friends
with you, if you'll be friends with me.

    [NERISSA *puts their hands together, and* PORTIA *kisses*
      BASSANIO.]

PORTIA. Have either of you seen my cousin?

NERISSA. Is he not with your other guests?

PORTIA. No. I came to take him to the masque.

NERISSA. He'll come presently. Meantime, we'll tell you of our plan to entertain him. Bassanio heard him say he'd like to see you in your lawyer's robes.

PORTIA. My lawyer's robes!

NERISSA. Those that you wore in Venice when Antonio was tried. And I bethought me of a little comedy we'd play to please him.

PORTIA. Yes?

NERISSA. We'll try Antonio a second time, and you. shall show your cousin how you won his case.

PORTIA. But Shylock's here! . . .

BASSANIO. Why must we always think of Shylock? . . .

NERISSA. He is not here—in this room. He's in another room, and will not see our play or even know of it.

PORTIA. Do you think my cousin will be pleased with this?

NERISSA. He told Bassanio so.

PORTIA. Then you have spoke to him about it.

NERISSA. We have. Is it not so, my lord.

BASSANIO. It is.

NERISSA. You have your robes still?

PORTIA. I keep them in my chamber, and sometimes, when I am alone, I put them on and am a man again. And your robes, too, Nerissa, I have them safe. You'll be my clerk!

NERISSA. No, no, clerking's a poor, unprofitable trade. I got Gratiano for my pay! . . .

PORTIA. Hush, hush, Nerissa! To-night's a festival. Forget you have a husband.

BASSANIO. Can you remember what you said before the Duke?

PORTIA. As much as I shall need. Come, Nerissa, let's get ready for the play. We'll show my cousin how we once were men.

[*Exeunt.*

BASSANIO. Now for the Jew! Where's Gratiano? (*He sees* BALTHASAR.) Balthasar! Balthasar!

BALTHASAR (*entering*). My lord!

BASSANIO. Find Gratiano for me.

BALTHASAR. Here he comes, my lord!

[*Enter* GRATIANO, *followed by* ANTONIO.

BASSANIO. She has agreed. Nerissa and she have gone to robe themselves. Has Gratiano told you, Antonio, what we plan?

ANTONIO. He has, and I dislike it.

BASSANIO. That's no matter. What's next to do?

GRATIANO. Get Shylock here to listen to the play.

BASSANIO. Balthasar, go to Shylock's chamber and bid him come to us here.

GRATIANO. Tell him your mistress desires to speak to him.

BALTHASAR. I will, my lord, but Doctor Bellario is with him now.

BASSANIO. Doctor Bellario!

ANTONIO. I suspect your cousin, Bassanio, I suspect him. He is a lawyer, and all lawyers are suspectable.

BASSANIO (*to* BALTHASAR). Go and tell Shylock what I have bid you. (BALTHASAR *goes out*.) What can Bellario be saying to him now?

GRATIANO. Bassanio, be civil to the Jew when he arrives. Rude words and frowning looks will not prevail with him.

ANTONIO. But if Portia sees him here, she will not consent to play!

GRATIANO. There'll be no play. When he sees her, the sight will be sufficient. He'll go in dudgeon, and that's what Bassanio wants.

BASSANIO. We'll have some sport with this performance, Gratiano.

GRATIANO. And bait the Jew a second time.

ANTONIO. I do not like this game! . . . (*He is about to go out*.)

BASSANIO. Stay here with us, Antonio.

ANTONIO. I am not anxious to meet Shylock without a larger company.

BASSANIO. He will not harm you, man. Stand by. Gratiano, go and tell our guests what we propose and bring them here.

GRATIANO. They'll throng to it. (*Exit*.)

BASSANIO. I'll make myself the master of this house before the night is out. (*Enter* BALTHASAR.) Well, sir?

BALTHASAR. My lord, Shylock bids me say he is not well and begs to be excused! . . .

BASSANIO. Return and tell him we'll not detain him long. The matter is important.

BALTHASAR. I will, my lord, but his words were firm.

BASSANIO. Let yours be firmer. Stay! Was Doctor Bellario with him when you left?

BALTHASAR. Not now, my lord.

BASSANIO. Where is he, then?

BALTHASAR. I do not know, my lord.

BASSANIO. When you have brought Shylock here, go and find him.

BALTHASAR. Yes, my lord. (*Exit.*)

    [GRATIANO, *followed by the guests, enters. There is a sound of talk and laughter mingled.* JESSICA *goes to* BASSANIO.]

JESSICA. What is it, Bassanio?

BASSANIO. A game, my dear!

JESSICA. I beg you, do not bait my father.

BASSANIO. There'll be no baiting. Stay here or go, which pleases you.

JESSICA. I'll go, my lord. I cannot stay and see him baited thus.

BASSANIO. Wait for me in the garden, near the gate. When this is done, I'll come to you. (*Exit* JESSICA.) (BASSANIO *joins the guests.*) Are you acquainted with our purpose?

A GENTLEMAN. Gratiano has told us of it.

A LADY. This will be the merriest masque of all.

ANTONIO. Indeed, I hope it will. I did not like it much when it was last performed.

BASSANIO. I pray you, gentles all, group yourselves about the room and leave the centre free.

GRATIANO. But where's the Jew?

BALTHASAR. I've sent for him. Are Portia and Nerissa ready?

A GENTLEMAN. I see them coming.

BASSANIO. Go, Gratiano, and bid them stay outside until we send for them. (GRATIANO *goes out.*) All you, my friends, have heard of how Antonio here, once a merchant in Venice, came near to losing his life! . . .

                [*Murmurs of sarcastic assent.*

A YOUNG MAN. We have, indeed, Bassanio, and feel

SHYLOCK.   But in those robes ! . . . Are you my judge ?

PORTIA.   I was your judge.

GRATIANO.   An upright judge, Jew ; a Daniel, a Daniel come to judgment.   O, Jew, do you remember now ?

SHYLOCK (to PORTIA).   I did not know.   I pray you, give me leave to go from hence.

[*Enter* DOCTOR BELLARIO.

PORTIA.   A moment, sir, I beg. (*To* BELLARIO.) Cousin Bellario, was it by your design that this play-acting was done ?

BELLARIO.   What play-acting ?

BASSANIO.   'Twas my design.

PORTIA.   Yours !   My lord, I ask no more from you than this, that if there be gentility in you, you show some signs of it.

BASSANIO.   I am your husband ! . . .

PORTIA.   I'm glad you have remembered that, for I had near forgot it.   But know, my lord, whether you be my husband or my harpy ! . . .

BASSANIO.   Harpy !

BELLARIO.   Cousin !

PORTIA.   The word I used was " harpy."   Whiche'er you be, my lord, I still am mistress of this house.   You have insulted this old man ! . . .

BELLARIO.   Insulted him !

PORTIA.   And made me party to the insult, and I demand that you shall here before our guests apologize to him.

BASSANIO.   Apologize !

BELLARIO.   What has happened ?   Will no one explain ?

BASSANIO.   I'll see him dead and damned ere I apologize.

SHYLOCK.   Madam, I am a stranger here and have no claim on your consideration.   Presently, I shall be gone. I beg you, leave this quarrel with your husband.

PORTIA.   Sir, I beg your pardon for the wrong you've suffered here to-night.   What was done was not by my desire.

BASSANIO.   But it was done with mine.   Get out, you Jew !

PORTIA.   Bassanio !   Leave my house !

[*There is consternation among the guests.*

BASSANIO.   Leave this . . . house !

BELLARIO.   Portia, your guests are troubled by their presence at this quarrel. (*To the Guests*.) My cousin will not feel aggrieved if you withdraw. (*Some of them move away*.)

PORTIA.   I beg you not to go, until my husband has repaired the wrong he's done.

BELLARIO.   Nay, please, all of you, go and leave us to settle this tedious dispute.

ANTONIO.   Does that mean me ?

BELLARIO.   Yes, you especially.

BASSANIO.   One moment, all !   You've heard me ordered from my home because I do not choose to have this gentleman my guest.   Well, since I'm ordered out, I'll go ! . . .

BELLARIO.   Bassanio, be reasonable ! . . .

BASSANIO.   Reasonable !   I, a Christian gentleman, am banished by my wife that she may gratify a Jew who could not keep his faith ! . . .

SHYLOCK.   My faith !

BASSANIO.   Who could not keep his faith, but went shivering to a Christian Church, lest he should lose his money or his life.   There's a fine Jew for you !   There's a faithful, upright, honest Jew.

SHYLOCK.   O, this is excess of misery !

BASSANIO.   I beg you, gentles, tell me what sort of Jew is he that changes his religion to save his skin.   Would one of you deny the Christ to keep his little hoard of money and his life ?

OMNES.   No, no, no !   We'd die first.   The man's a traitor to his faith !

BASSANIO.   Did not our fathers sweat in bloody war to keep their faith ?   And are not we, men and women, aye, and children too, ready to give our lives for it ? (*Shouts of agreement*.)   But what Jew will fight for his ? What Jew will fight for anything ?   Has any Jew a country he will die for ?

PORTIA.   My lord, you have not died for yours !

BASSANIO.   Peace, woman !   I'll say what's in my mind. There is no Jew will fight.   There is no country that a Jew will die for, and we see here how soon a Jew will change his faith if that will bring him profit and security. But is that all we Christians want ?   Are we poor, crawling

BASSANIO. Come gentles, let us go. This house will presently become a synagogue, and we, being Christians, will be foreign here. Gratiano, we'll continue our festival in your Christian home.

GRATIANO. We will, my lord. I'll warrant you there'll be no Jews in my house. Where is the wench with whom I danced?

A GIRL. I'm here, Gratiano.

GRATIANO (*embracing her*). You'll come and dance with me!

NERISSA. Husband! Gratiano!

GRATIANO. Puff! puff! old sourface!

BASSANIO. Come, then!

[BASSANIO *and* GRATIANO, *with the girl between them, go out, followed by the guests.* NERISSA, *baulked and angry, stands for a moment.*]

NERISSA (*aside*). I know what plans Bassanio has with Jessica. Lorenzo'll hear of this. (*Exit.*)

ANTONIO. I'm sorry, Portia! . . .

[*She does not answer, and, after a moment of bewilderment, he goes out too.*]

BELLARIO. This is a distressing matter. Your husband is an obstinate, but eloquent man, Portia. I had arranged with Shylock here that he should lend you money! . . .

PORTIA. Lend me money!

BELLARIO. Yes, and very reasonably, too.

PORTIA. O, I am humiliated! (*To* SHYLOCK.) Sir, what can I say to you?

SHYLOCK. Nothing! Say nothing! There is nothing to say. I pray you, send for your husband and make peace with him. I'll leave you now. There is a fellow here will take me to my daughter's house, and when that's done, I'll go to Venice. You will not see me again. Make peace, then, with your husband.

PORTIA. Good-night, Shylock!

SHYLOCK. Good-night, Portia!

[*He picks up his cloak and goes out.*

THE FOURTH ACT

A bedroom in the house of LORENZO *and* JESSICA.
*There is a wide window at the back of the scene,
overlooking the garden. On the spectator's right is a
narrow door, near the front of the scene, which leads
along a short passage to the room where* LORENZO
and JESSICA'S *children sleep. On the spectator's left,
in the middle of the wall, is a larger door leading to the
rest of the house.*

> [*The scene is in darkness, except for moonlight,
> when the curtain rises, but almost immediately
> LAUNCELOT GOBBO, carrying a lamp and followed
> by SHYLOCK, enters.*]

GOBBO.   This is their room, sir !

SHYLOCK.   Where are my grandsons ?

GOBBO.   Hush, sir ! Do not speak so loud.   (*He points
to the small door.*)   They are in that room.   There is a
little passage which leads to it. . . .

SHYLOCK (*interrupting him*).   Let us go into it quickly,
then !

GOBBO.   Stay, sir ! I'll go first and see if they are
asleep.

> [*He opens the little door and goes through the passage to
> the room where the children are.* SHYLOCK *stands
> in silence until he returns.*]

GOBBO.   They are asleep.   I listened to their breathing.
Come, sir, but be quiet, if you please, lest they wake.

SHYLOCK.   And why should they not wake ? May a man
not speak with his grandsons ?

GOBBO.   Nay, sir, if you will not behave with discretion,
I will not let you go to them at all.   You must promise

GOBBO. O, miserable Gobbo! Miserable, miserable Gobbo! This is what comes of being kind. I may as well hang myself now or marry the fat innkeeper, for I'll get a poor greeting from my lord when he hears of this. I'll go! I'll not wait! I'll spend the night with friends and say I ne'er came home at all, and if the brat blabs to his father, I'll swear he dreamt it all. I'll get so drunk that I'll have a hundred witnesses to prove I was not here to-night. Farewell, Jew! Farewell, Christians that should be Jews! Farewell, everything! And now I'll go and souse myself!

[*He goes out. The door of the children's chamber opens, and* SHYLOCK, *carrying the light, reappears.*]

SHYLOCK. Gobbo! (*He comes into the centre of the room.*) Gobbo!

[YOUNG LORENZO *appears in the doorway.*

YOUNG LORENZO. Where's Gobbo?

SHYLOCK. I think he must have gone. (*He puts the lamp down and seats himself.*) Come, here, Lorenzo!

[*The boy climbs on to his knee again.*

YOUNG LORENZO. Why did Gobbo go? It's so funny to leave me alone with a stranger!

SHYLOCK. A stranger!

YOUNG LORENZO. Yes. You're a stranger!

SHYLOCK. I'm a stranger! Tell me, Lorenzo, has no one ever told you about your grandfather?

YOUNG LORENZO. Oh, yes! He's dead!

SHYLOCK. Dead! Who is dead?

YOUNG LORENZO. My grandfather! His name was Lorenzo, too!

SHYLOCK. Oh, that grandfather!

YOUNG LORENZO. We are the three Lorenzos: my grandfather, my father, and me!

SHYLOCK. But you have another one, your mother's father?

YOUNG LORENZO. Oh, yes, but he lives a long way off. He's a foreigner, not quite like us!

SHYLOCK. And you never see him?

YOUNG LORENZO. No.

SHYLOCK. Do you never wish to see him?

YOUNG LORENZO. Father and mother do not like to speak about him.

SHYLOCK. Why?

YOUNG LORENZO. I don't know. What a funny old man you are! You keep on asking questions.

SHYLOCK. Don't you ever think of your other grandfather?

YOUNG LORENZO. Sometimes. Not often. Do you know, Launcelot Gobbo told me once that my other grandfather is a Jew!

SHYLOCK. Did he? And what did you say to that?

YOUNG LORENZO. I hit him with my whip, and then I told my father what he had said, and father was very angry and beat him again. He got two beatings for that. Of course, poor Gobbo was drunk, but he ought not to have said such a thing.

SHYLOCK. Why, my dear?

YOUNG LORENZO. Well, would you like to be told that your grandfather was a Jew, even if you'd never seen him?

SHYLOCK. My grandfather was a Jew.

YOUNG LORENZO. Oh! Then you are a Jew?

SHYLOCK. I am . . . a sort of a Jew.

YOUNG LORENZO. But I thought all Jews were wicked people. You're kind.

SHYLOCK. Do you like me, Lorenzo?

YOUNG LORENZO. I think so. Yes, I do.

[SHYLOCK *hugs the boy to him, and there is silence for a moment or two.*]

YOUNG LORENZO. I'm so sleepy now.

SHYLOCK. Are you? Shall I take you back to bed?

YOUNG LORENZO. Will you tell me a story first?

SHYLOCK. I do not know many stories.

YOUNG LORENZO. Gobbo knows a lot. (*He yawns.*) Oh, dear, I'm so tired!

SHYLOCK. Lie close to me! . . .

[*The boy snuggles down into* SHYLOCK'S *arms, making little childish noises of content as he does so.*]

YOUNG LORENZO (*in a sleepy voice*). Go on! Tell me a story!

SHYLOCK. There was once an old man . . .

YOUNG LORENZO. Yes.

SHYLOCK. Who was very lonely. And he started off one day on a journey . . .

YOUNG LORENZO. Was it a long journey?

SHYLOCK. A very long journey. He wanted to find someone he loved and to see some little children that he had never seen! . . .

YOUNG LORENZO. Yes.

SHYLOCK. And when he had travelled a long while he came to a place where he found a little boy . . .

YOUNG LORENZO. Like me?

SHYLOCK. Just like you!

YOUNG LORENZO. It isn't a very amusing story!

SHYLOCK. No, no, it isn't an amusing story!

YOUNG LORENZO. Don't you know anything funny or exciting?

SHYLOCK. I'll try and think of something.

YOUNG LORENZO. I'll keep quiet while you think. Shall I?

SHYLOCK. Yes. Do.

[*They are silent for a moment or two. Then* SHYLOCK *sees that the boy is asleep. He gathers him up in his arms and carries him very gently to the children's bedroom.*

After a few moments, the outer door opens, and JESSICA *enters. She glances around the room and sees that the children's door is open. She goes to it, listens a moment, but hears nothing. She shuts the door and goes to the window, which she opens, and leans out.*]

JESSICA. Bassanio!

BASSANIO (*in the garden*). Jessica!

JESSICA. Hush! All's quiet, but make no noise!

BASSANIO. I'll climb this way!

JESSICA. Take care, my lord!

BASSANIO. This is a trifle, Jessica, to me.

[*She moves to the side of the window, and as she does so,* BASSANIO *appears.*]

JESSICA. Oh, my lord!

[BASSANIO *swings himself over the sill into the room.*

BASSANIO. Why, what's ado?

JESSICA. I was afraid you'd fall.

BASSANIO. Fall! My dear, I've often done this before.
Come!

[He takes her in his arms and embraces her.

BASSANIO. Little blackbird!

JESSICA. Do you truly love me, Bassanio?

BASSANIO. Truly I do. (*Kissing her.*) Little blackbird! I love your deep, dark hair! . . .

JESSICA. Portia has golden hair.

BASSANIO. She has. I loved it once.

JESSICA. You do not love it now?

BASSANIO. How can a man love anything continuously?
Kiss me!

[He pulls her to him and kisses her.

JESSICA. Will you not love me continuously?

BASSANIO. I'll love you as long as I can. No one can
promise more. An active gentleman that has his health
and strength, when there are no wars, must have variety
of love. I'll not pretend, Jessica, that I will always be
faithful to you, for that's impossible, but I'll be faithful to
you as long as I can! I have loved fair women and dark
women and tall women and little women, and women that
were fierce and women that were gentle, but I have never
loved one woman only. I have a wide heart, Jessica, with
room for many sorts of women.

JESSICA. I'd have you love me only.

BASSANIO. They all say that. But what an arrogance
it is to deem yourself so high above all others that there's
no thought left for anyone but you? I do not think
myself unique. Then why do you think you're
unique?

JESSICA. Will you be tolerant then if Portia takes a
lover?

BASSANIO. No, by God! But I'm a man, and she's a
woman.

JESSICA. I am a woman, and Lorenzo is a man.

BASSANIO. No, Lorenzo's a poet. Besides, all logic
breaks down somewhere. Mine breaks down here. I'll
take another's wife, but heaven help him that takes
mine.

JESSICA. I care not, so that you love me.

BASSANIO. I do.

JESSICA. Then take me! . . .
  [*The door of the children's chamber opens and* SHYLOCK
      enters.]
BASSANIO. Good God, what's that?
JESSICA. My father!
BASSANIO. God's blood, the everlasting Jew!
                              [SHYLOCK *comes close to them.*
SHYLOCK. I hardly thought to find you here, my lord!
BASSANIO. Your presence surprises me as much as
mine surprises you. Did you arrange this, Jessica?
JESSICA. No, my lord! Father, how came you here?
SHYLOCK. I had a longing to see my grandsons, and
while you danced Gobbo brought me here.
JESSICA. Gobbo!
BASSANIO. I'll kill Gobbo.
SHYLOCK. Your sons are sleeping, Jessica.
JESSICA. Did you speak to them?
SHYLOCK. I spoke to young Lorenzo. He does not
know who I am. I'll go now, and perhaps Bassanio will
conduct me to an inn.
BASSANIO. I'll not conduct you! . . .
SHYLOCK. It would be unmannerly of me to leave you
with my daughter when her husband is not here.
BASSANIO. I'll pardon the unmannerliness.
SHYLOCK. But yet I cannot go unless you do me honour
and come with me.
BASSANIO. I do not walk with Jews! . . .
SHYLOCK. My daughter is a Jewess.
BASSANIO. Much is forgiven to women.
SHYLOCK. You hate Jews?
BASSANIO. Like Hell!
SHYLOCK. Do you hate Hell? And take so little care to
keep out of it?
BASSANIO. I am not in a mood for pleasantries. I beg
you, take your leave.
SHYLOCK. While you remain here? My lord, though
I'm a Jew, I have a father's heart. Jessica, I gave you
all the love my heart could hold, and you betrayed me for a
man that hated me. Now, I find you betraying him!
BASSANIO. Come, come! . . .
SHYLOCK. Silence, my lord. I am this woman's father.
There is a legend of our race that wives and husbands

shall be faithful to each other, whatever comes to them, and I have always held it dear. You have despised me for my race, and I have borne your contempt as best I could. But here's a different cause, my lord. I love my daughter, though she loves me not, and hold her faithfulness and honour as a trust, although her husband keeps my name concealed from her children's ears. And so I bid you, lord Bassanio, leave this house.

BASSANIO. You bid me ! . . .

SHYLOCK. I bid you leave this house, and leave it now.

BASSANIO. I'll see you damned, and damned again ! . . .

[*A single loud knock is heard on the street door.*

JESSICA. Hush ! What's that ?

[*They remain silent. The knock is repeated.* JESSICA *hesitates. Then she goes towards the door.*]

JESSICA. I pray you go, my lord, and you, father, go, too.

BASSANIO. Why, what's to do ? We can conceal ourselves, if there is need.

JESSICA. If it should be Lorenzo ! . . .

BASSANIO. But he's in France, or thereabouts !

JESSICA. I fear this knocking bodes no good. I beg you, dear Bassanio, go.

SHYLOCK. How shall I depart ?

JESSICA. There's no way now but by the window.

SHYLOCK. I am not skilled in window-work.

[*The knock is heard for the third time.*

JESSICA. He knocks again. I beg you, go ! . . .

BASSANIO. If there is need, we'll hide ourselves. Go now and see who 'tis.

[JESSICA *goes out.*

BASSANIO. The hour is late for visitors.

SHYLOCK You did not find it so, my lord.

BASSANIO. My visit, good Jew, was not a ceremonial one. However, I am not here to bandy jokes with you.

SHYLOCK. I suspected that, my lord.

BASSANIO. Be silent a moment. (*He listens at the door.*)

SHYLOCK. What do you hear ?

BASSANIO. What can I hear with you chattering ? . . . (*He listens hard and hears the voice of* PORTIA.) My God, my wife !

SHYLOCK. Who ?

LORENZO.   Who was it then?

BALTHASAR.   I think it was a man.

LORENZO (*slamming the window to*).   Hell and damnation! (*Coming into the room.*)   You had best be honest, madam.   Who was it came?

JESSICA.   My lord, you do me wrong.   'Twas no one, that I swear!

PORTIA.   What became of the man Balthasar saw at the window?   Did he escape?

LORENZO.   I had forgot that. (*He goes to the window again.*)   Balthasar!

BALTHASAR.   My lord!

LORENZO.   Did this man you saw at the window leave by it?

BALTHASAR.   No, my lord.

LORENZO.   Then he's still here!

JESSICA.   No, no, my lord, he's not.

PORTIA.   Then he *was* here?

JESSICA.   No, no, I do not mean that he was here.   You put confusion in my mouth.   Lorenzo, husband, no one was here, no one's here now.   I swear it that am your loving wife.

PORTIA (*pointing to the door that leads to the children's room*).   What door is that?

JESSICA.   My children's room.

PORTIA.   He may be there.

JESSICA (*interrupting them*).   My children are asleep. You'll frighten them as you have frightened me.

LORENZO.   Stand aside.

JESSICA (*kneeling before him and clasping him round the knees*).   My lord Lorenzo, if you have ever loved me, trust me now, I beg you.

LORENZO.   I'll trust no more.   Give me leave.

JESSICA.   I will not let you go! . . .

LORENZO.   Then must I make you! . . .

[*He throws her aside and she falls heavily on the floor. His sword is out, and he makes a step towards the door.   As he does so, it opens and* SHYLOCK *enters.*]

LORENZO.   Shylock!

SHYLOCK.   Lorenzo!

PORTIA. You!

SHYLOCK. My lady!

LORENZO. What means this? (*To* JESSICA.) How comes the Jew here?

SHYLOCK. I am her father, and hearing she had children, I had a wish to see them.

JESSICA. I did not bring him here, Lorenzo.

SHYLOCK. No, she did not bring me. I came against her will, without her knowledge. When she returned from Portia's house, she found me here, and while she was rebuking me, you came. Her heart's a timorous one, and when she heard the knocking at your door she was afraid 'twas you returning, and lest you might be angry with her for harbouring me, her father, and letting me see your children, my grandsons, she begged me to conceal myself. And so I did.

LORENZO. And you were here alone with her?

SHYLOCK. I was.

PORTIA. Was not my husband here?

SHYLOCK. No.

LORENZO. Oh, Jessica! (*He lifts her from the floor and holds her in his arms.*) I have wronged you deeply, Jessica.

[*She does not answer, but weeps lavishly on his breast while he comforts her.*]

SHYLOCK. A daughter's heart's a tender thing, Lorenzo. Affection for her father, despised of you, brought her to this. Use her kindly.

PORTIA. I've done you wrong, Jessica. I beg you'll pardon me.

LORENZO. Look up, my love!

JESSICA. It's hard, my lady, but I do forgive you.

PORTIA. I'll leave you now. Lorenzo, will you conduct me to the street?

LORENZO. I'll bid Balthasar meet you at the door (*He goes to the window and calls to* BALTHASAR.)

BALTHASAR. My lord!

LORENZO. Go to the front of the house and meet your mistress there. All's well here!

BALTHASAR. What shall I do with Gobbo, my lord?

LORENZO. Let him go, and bid him not come near this house again. (*He shuts the window.*) I am glad for

THE FIFTH ACT

The scene is laid in PORTIA'S *garden. The time is the next morning, and the garden is bright and sunny and full of flowers.* PORTIA *is sitting under a tree, apparently reading a book, but in reality she is listening to* STEPHANO *who, invisible to the audience as yet, is singing somewhere near at hand a song which he learned from his father. It is :*

> Tell me where is fancy bred,
>> Or in the heart or in the head ?
> How begot, how nourished ?
>> Reply, reply.
> It is engendered in the eyes,
> With gazing fed ; and fancy dies
> In the cradle where it lies.
>> Let us all ring fancy's knell ;
>> I'll begin it, Ding, dong, bell.

[*He enters, his arms full of flowers and green stuff, as he sings the last two lines.*]

PORTIA. Stephano !

STEPHANO. My lady !

PORTIA. Who taught you that song ?

STEPHANO. My father, madam, when he was your servant.

PORTIA. I remember. He sang it when Bassanio came to choose the caskets.

STEPHANO. These flowers are for your chamber, my lady. I gathered them myself.

PORTIA. Thank you, Stephano.

STEPHANO. I'll take them to the house now.

PORTIA. Do.

[*He goes out, and as he goes he is heard singing, " Tell
me where is fancy bred ! " The sound of his singing
dies away.* PORTIA *sits back in her seat, but does not
read. She is thinking of what happened in* JESSICA'S
bedroom last night. BALTHASAR *enters.*]

BALTHASAR. My lady ! . . .

PORTIA (*interrupting him*). Has your lord returned ?

BALTHASAR. I have not seen him, my lady.

PORTIA. I thought perhaps he had returned. Well ?

BALTHASAR. Lord Lorenzo and his lady and the old
gentleman from Venice ! . . .

PORTIA. Shylock ?

BALTHASAR. Yes, my lady ! They are within the house
and wish to speak to you.

PORTIA. Bring them here.

BALTHASAR. I will, my lady !

[*He goes out. Hardly has he done so when* BASSANIO,
still unaware that Portia saw him drop from
JESSICA'S *window, enters by the same way that*
STEPHANO *came.*]

BASSANIO. Portia !

PORTIA. You have returned, my lord !

BASSANIO. Yes. I learned an hour ago that after I
had gone you sent the Jew fellow packing, and so I have
returned, willing to forgive and to forget.

PORTIA. I am obliged to you, my lord !

BASSANIO. We'll say no more about it.

PORTIA. That, perhaps, will be best.

BASSANIO. Provided that the Jew does not return! . . .

PORTIA. I'm afraid he's here already !

BASSANIO. What ! Again ?

PORTIA. Balthasar has just told me of his arrival. I'm
waiting for him now.

BASSANIO. The fellow will take possession of the house
if we're not careful. You must tell him to go ! . . .

PORTIA. I'm afraid that's not possible, my lord !

BASSANIO. Now, look here, Portia, once and for all
this question of authority must be settled. A house
which is divided against itself must fall.

BASSANIO. Attempts! What attempts? Who has told this calumny of me? Was it this Jew here? . . .

SHYLOCK. You forget, my lord, that I came to Belmont yesterday after he had gone, and was too much occupied with your attentions to me to think about my son-in-law.

PORTIA. Poor Jessica is all a blur of tears. I fear our talk distresses her. When innocence is wronged, the hurt is deeper than when guilt's discovered. Do we annoy you, Jessica, with all this flippant talk?

JESSICA. I would rather not hear it.

PORTIA. Your desire is natural. But, Bassanio has not heard all, and since he's concerned as much as you, he ought to know the whole story. That's fair and just, is it not, Jessica? (*A sob from* JESSICA.) But I'll be brief. Listen, Bassanio! Lorenzo hurried here and told his story to me, after you had left last night, and I, to humour him, for, indeed, I did not doubt you, my lord, went with him to his house, where we found Jessica alone.

BASSANIO. Then I was not there?

PORTIA. No, you were not visible; I mean you were not there.

BASSANIO. Ha! Well, you must have frightened Jessica with your rude suspicions! What did you do, Jessica?

JESSICA. I wept.

PORTIA. That was right. We should always weep when we are doubted.

BASSANIO. You used her ill, Lorenzo.

LORENZO. I know, and am ashamed to think of it. (*He embraces* JESSICA.)

PORTIA. But listen to what follows, my lord. There *was* a man in Jessica's room.

BASSANIO. Was! . . .

PORTIA. Balthasar saw him. Balthasar's eyes are strong.

BASSANIO. Balthasar!

PORTIA. Our steward! You remember our steward, my lord? He saw the man and can identify him.

BASSANIO. Oh! Who was the man?

PORTIA. Can you not guess?

BASSANIO. How can I guess? I do not know what men frequent her room?

LORENZO. Bassanio!

PORTIA. A joke, Lorenzo. A poor joke, but his own !
It is an easy thing to guess, Bassanio. What man should
be in her room ?

BASSANIO. Lorenzo !

PORTIA. Well answered ! Well answered, Bassanio !
Yet it was not her husband. Come, guess, my lord !

BASSANIO. I am not good at riddles. Who was it ?

PORTIA. Why, her father ! Shylock !

SHYLOCK. It was, my lord !

PORTIA. Is that not funny, Bassanio ? We went to find
a lover in her room, and found a grandfather tendering his
grandsons !

BASSANIO. Ha ! Ha, ha, ha !

PORTIA. It is funny, is it not, Bassanio ?

BASSANIO (*more confident now*). Oh, very funny, very
funny ! Ha, ha, ha ! Eh, Lorenzo, is this not a comical
tale ? You went out to be a cuckold and found yourself a
son-in-law ! . . .

PORTIA. That was much more satisfactory, wasn't
it, Bassanio ?

BASSANIO. By God, yes ! Ha, ha, ha ! Come, old Jew,
you must see the humour of that.

SHYLOCK. Yes, I think I see it.

BASSANIO. Well, why don't you laugh, then ? You
know, Shylock, a Jew can't see a joke. Your race is too
literal ! That's what's the matter with it. You took the
Old Testament much too seriously, Shylock, and that's
why you lost the New one. Portia told me that, and it's
true. You were all so busy looking for a common king to
come and rule over you, that you didn't notice God, and
that's an oversight that's going to cost you dear. Here,
Jessica, come and confide in me ! Was there not a lover
in the cupboard all the time ?

JESSICA. O, my lord !

LORENZO. Bassanio, this is unworthy of you !

BASSANIO. Come, come, Lorenzo, let's have our jest
out ! What, Jessica ?

JESSICA. No, Bassanio, there was no one in the room
but my father !

BASSANIO. No gallant gentleman, like me, to whisper
endearments to you while Lorenzo went abroad ?

I was a bitter-minded man, and cherished hatred in my heart. Sometimes, still, I am full of anger when I hear my race derided. What have we Jews done that we should be loathed and mocked by all mankind?

PORTIA. You would not acknowledge God, but crucified Him.

SHYLOCK. And have not all men crucified Him? Yet all men are not damned as Jews are damned! When I was left in Venice, after Jessica had fled and all my goods and lands were taken from me, I sat in my hungry house and thought of this many times, but never found an answer to my questions, till I learned that we're despised by you because you are despised by us. We are a proud and narrow race, and our pride and narrow minds have ruined us. I have the power to govern men. Here in my breast I feel the power to govern men. My heart stirs when I think of generous government and of kindly races striving each with each for greater love and beauty and finer men and women. But I'm condemned, because I am a Jew, to be a usurer and spend my mind on little furtive schemes for making money.

PORTIA. You have no roots. Your race is shallow in its growth.

SHYLOCK. Yet we are old.

PORTIA. All mankind is old. It's only governments are new. You were a nomad race in Israel, shifting like your own sand; and you're still a nomad race, rootless, unstable, blown by self-interest round the world, with no place that's your own. There is no hope for Jews, Shylock, till they have learned to share the lot of all of us, to live and, if there be the need, to die for some poor soil they call their native land.

SHYLOCK. We cannot go back, madam—we must go on and mingle with the world and lose ourselves in other men. I know that outward things pass and have no duration. There is nothing left but the goodness which a man performs. And so, I take my son and my daughter and their children back to Venice, because their going may take some harm away from you.

[STEPHANO *is heard, at a distance, singing the song:* " *Come, master youth, count up your charity.*"]

PORTIA.   And you forgive all that we have done to you ?

SHYLOCK.   I must forgive. We must all forgive, because we have so much to be forgiven.

PORTIA.   Let us go in !

[SHYLOCK *offers her his arm, and she takes it. They listen for a moment to* STEPHANO'S *song, which grows louder as he approaches. Then they go in together;* STEPHANO, *still unseen, sings his song to the end. The play is finished.*]